CASH ON DELIVERY

First produced in London by Bill Kenwright in association with Ray Cooney and Proscenium A. S. at the Whitehall Theatre, on 18th September 1996, with the following cast:

Eric Swan	Bradley Walsh
Linda Swan	Tracie Bennett
Norman Bassett	Nick Wilton
Mr Jenkins	Frank Thornton
Uncle George	Brian Murphy
Sally Chessington	Anita Graham
Doctor Chapman	Justin Shevlan
Mr Forbright	John Hart Dyke
Ms Cowper	Jean Fergusson
Miss Dixon	Fenella Shepherd

Directed by Ray Cooney
Designed by Douglas Heap
Lighting by Kevin Grainger

Setting — The living-room of 344 Chilton Road, just off the Mile End Road in East London

Time — Just after 9 a.m. on a windy October morning. The action is continuous

Cash On Delivery

A Comedy

Michael Cooney

Samuel French — London
New York - Toronto - Hollywood

ISBN 0 573 01752 2

Please see page iv for further copyright information

Designer: Douglas Heap

ACT I

The action of the play takes place in the living-room of 344 Chilton Road, just off the Mile End Road in East London. It is just after nine o'clock on a windy, rainy October morning

It is a tastefully, but not extravagantly, refurbished Victorian house belonging to Eric Swan and his wife Linda. There is a solid front door UC (*large brass numbers 344, with a letter box but no glass) and a small porch outside the front door.* L *of the front door is a bay window, that looks out on to the houses opposite. This window has a window-seat in front, with a hinged lid just large enough to hide a body. There is an umbrella stand by the door. An archway* UR *leads to the stairs (the bottom few steps are visible, the stairs open out to a small landing, which in turn would lead to the upstairs flat, belonging to the Swans' lodger, Norman Bassett).* UL, *a door leads through to the dining-room and* DL *a door leads to the kitchen (cabinets are visible off-stage). There is a small cupboard above the* UL *dining-room door, which blends unobtrusively into the framing of the door.* DR *a door leads to the ground floor bedroom of Eric and Linda. All doors open out on to the stage. A new sofa* DR/C *has an end table at its* SL *with a push-button phone. There is a chair against the* L *wall, between the kitchen and dining-room doors. The few paintings, although pleasing, are there for wall covering rather than artistic appreciation. There is a clock on the wall between the bedroom door and the* UR *arch*

The CURTAIN *rises on an empty stage. All the doors are closed and it is raining*

Linda enters from the bedroom drinking coffee from a mug. She is wearing a smart suit

Linda Eric! Eric, darling!

Eric enters from the kitchen (leaving the door open), hiding the cordless phone from his wife. He is wearing the trousers of a suit and a plain shirt

Eric Yes, love?
Linda Have you got the house keys?
Eric You locked up last night, didn't you, love?
Linda Maybe they're in the kitchen.
Eric Yes.

She moves past him towards the kitchen, but turns back to give him a "good-morning" kiss

Linda then exits into the kitchen (leaving the door open)

Eric reveals the phone he's been hiding, puts it to his ear and shuts the kitchen door

Eric (*on the phone*) You still there? ... Sorry about that — Now, have I reached the Department of Social Security? ... Excellent. I have to be quick. I want to cancel all my social security payments ...

Linda re-enters from the kitchen minus the coffee mug

Linda Not there!

Eric hastily puts the phone in his trouser pocket and sits nonchalantly on the settee

Maybe they're in my handbag.
Eric (*chuckling*) Yes, that's the last place you'd think of looking.
Linda (*chuckling*) All right!

Linda exits DR *into the bedroom*

Eric (*immediately back on the phone*) Sorry about that. ... Yes, cancel *all* my social security benefits. ... I need to speak to each division? ... Well, if you put me through to the Income Support Division, will they be able to forward me to the Family Benefit Division? ...

Linda re-enters

Linda I've found them.

Eric quickly shoves the phone down the front of his trousers. Linda puts on her coat

Right, let's go.
Eric Listen, darling. You go ahead. I'll catch up with you on the way to the station.
Linda But you'll miss our train.
Eric I'm not dressed yet and I wouldn't want to make you late for work.
Linda But what about you?
Eric Oh, I'll be all right. I'll borrow Norman's bike and leave it at the station.

Linda Norman will have already left for his shoe shop. Anyway, you can't just borrow the lodger's bike without asking.
Eric Then I'll jog to the station, the exercise will do me good.

Eric jogs on the spot for a moment — then suddenly thrusts his hands into his pockets to stop the phone slipping

Linda (*compassionately concerned*) Eric, everything is all right, isn't it?
Eric (*overly happy*) Yes. Everything's absolutely wonderful.
Linda I mean, you don't have any problems at the Electricity Board, do you?
Eric No. No, work's fine. (*Then, appearing offhand*) Are you worried about me for any reason?
Linda Oh no, nothing really.
Eric Good, good.
Linda But if there was anything wrong, you would talk to me, wouldn't you, Eric?

Linda tries to cuddle Eric — and he pushes his bottom out so that she doesn't notice the phone

Eric Of course I would, darling. And if you were worried, you'd talk to me, wouldn't you?
Linda Of course. So I've got nothing to worry about.
Eric Not a thing. Both of us. Nothing to worry about.
Linda Good. I'll meet you at the station then.
Eric I'll be five minutes behind you.
Linda (*making for the front door*) I'll be waiting.

Linda exits through the front door

The moment Linda leaves, Eric shakes his leg — the phone falls out of his trouser leg and he is quickly back on the phone

Eric (*on the phone*) Are you still there? ... Bloody music. "*Flight of the Bumble Bee*" at nine in the morning. (*Then*) Ah, hallo, which Division am I talking to? ... "Income Support". Excellent. Well, my name is Eric Swan, I'm phoning because of my upstairs lodger, Norman Bassett. ... No, that's "Norman", like the conquests ... and "Bassett", as in liquorice. ... Yes. Well, I believe Norman has been claiming unemployment benefit from you, is that correct? ... Yes, I thought so. Well, I just phoned to say that there's no need to send Norman's cheque for this week, or any further cheques for that matter. ... Er, no. No, Norman hasn't found a job. He died this morning. ... Yes, it came as a terrible shock to everybody here. ... That's

why I phoned. ... No, Norman died of natural causes. ... He's what? In line
for a funeral payment. No, you don't understand, I'm trying to *cancel* all
of his security payments. ... I don't care if he *is* eligible, he doesn't want it.
... No, his wife doesn't want a widow's payment. ... Nor extra child care.

Norman Bassett enters through the stairs archway into the living-room.
Although dressed, Norman's wrapped in a woollen blanket. But he's full
of bright energy, determined to shake off his cold

Eric doesn't notice Norman entering behind him

(*On the phone, giving in*) All right, all right — and will I have to pick up
one of those forms at the local DSS office?
Norman Morning, Eric!
Eric (*surprised*) Ha!
Norman Sorry, Eric. Didn't mean to startle you ...
Eric Norman! What are you doing here?
Norman I came down to borrow some pills.
Eric Why aren't you at the shoe shop? It's after nine.

Eric tries to interrupt during Norman's following speech ...

Norman Yes, I know. I woke up this morning feeling really lousy. Well, with
my wedding just three days away, I want to shake this thing off. You know
me and my nose, Eric. Just say the word "cold" and I can't keep my hands
off the Night Nurse. I mean I couldn't let my Brenda down, could I?
Eric Norman, can't you see that I'm on the phone? What do you want?
Norman I was wondering if Mrs Swan might have some aspirin in the
kitchen.
Eric Linda has just left for the station. But there may be something in there.
Help yourself. And Norman — don't sneak up on me again.

Eric hurries Norman out and closes the kitchen door

(*Straight back on the phone without wasting a moment*) I'm sorry about
that, it was — er — the late Norman Bassett's wife, I mean "widow". She's
crumbled, I'm afraid. ... Yes, usually she's the backbone of the Bassett
family. But she's in a terrible state. ... Norman's three children? Oh, well,
they're absolutely distraught. I can hear them all crying from here. (*He*
holds the phone away and makes a quick sobbing sound) Cause of death?
(*He takes out a scrap of paper from his pocket and reads*) Norman died of
"Lassa Fever". ... That's right, the doctor said it was very rare these days.

Norman enters from the kitchen, trying to get the top off a bottle of aspirin with his teeth. He crosses unnoticed to behind Eric again

(*On the phone*) Well, thank you. And I'll be certain to pass on your commiserations to Mrs Bassett. Most kind.

Norman Commiserations to Mrs Bassett?

Eric (*on the phone, quickly*) And I'll be sure to get all the necessaries in the post to you by the end of the week. Thank you and good-day.

Eric hangs up and starts towards the bedroom

Did you find what you were looking for?

Norman Who was that on the phone?

Eric Oh, just a lady from the local Women's Institute.

Again, Eric moves to the bedroom but is stopped by Norman

Norman Why was a lady from the Women's Institute sending her commiserations to my mother?

Eric I'd put your mum and dad into a raffle.

Norman Who'd want to win my mum and dad?

Eric As contestants.

Norman Oh.

Eric But they didn't win — that's why the WI was sending their commiserations. I mean, the top prize was a three-week world cruise. First-class cabin, Captain's table every night. It was for their golden wedding anniversary.

Norman Golden wedding anniversary. What a lovely thought, Eric. But they didn't win.

Eric No. They're getting the runners-up prize instead.

Norman Oh. And what's that, then?

Eric A toaster.

Norman A toaster. Not bad. Did you know your washing machine's making that funny noise again?

Eric (*not interested*) Is it? If you'll excuse me, Norman, I've got to get to the station. Oh, can I borrow your bike?

Norman Eric, I can't seem to get the lid off this bottle of aspirin.

Eric Let me have a look. (*He takes the bottle and glances at the label*) Here's your problem.

Norman What's that then?

Eric (*giving the bottle back*) Says right here on the label — idiot proof.

Norman gives Eric a stern look

Eric exits into the bedroom, leaving the door open

Norman You shouldn't talk to me like that, Eric. Not only have I been your lodger for the past two years, but you are to be Best Man at my wedding on Saturday. And I have been a loyal and trustworthy friend, through thick and thin, whenever you or Linda needed a shoulder to cry on ...

Eric appears from the bedroom

Eric You can't pay your rent again, can you?
Norman In a word, no. But I promise you, Eric, I'll have your money the moment Brenda and I return from our honeymoon.
Eric Fine.
Norman God, me on a honeymoon! It's amazing.
Eric Yes, it's quite a thought.
Norman Who'd have guessed three months ago that I'd attend a shoe salesman conference in Lyme Regis and come back with my future bride.
Eric It's certainly some feat.

Norman doesn't get the pun

Eric exits into the bedroom, closing the door

Norman When you and Linda meet Brenda on Saturday, you'll just fall in love with her. Everybody does. (*Then, to himself*) I did.

The doorbell chimes

I'll get it.

The doorbell chimes again

(*Calling*) Coming!

Norman opens the front door to reveal George Jenkins, a middle-aged council employee who is probably less intelligent than he thinks, standing in the doorway, clipboard and briefcase in hand

Good-morning.
Jenkins Yes, it is. A little showery, though. I apologize for disturbing you this early. I'm from the Department of Social Security. Sickness and Disability Division.
Norman Yes?

Jenkins Are you Mr Thompson?
Norman Er — no.
Jenkins Then will you tell Mr Thompson that I'm here to see him.
Norman I don't understand.
Jenkins Oh. Well, it's quite simple really. I'm a DSS Inspector and I'm here to see Mr Rupert Thompson.
Norman I think there must be some sort of a mistake.
Jenkins This is 344 Chilton Road, is it not?
Norman Yes.
Jenkins Then there shouldn't be any mistake.

Norman hesitates. Then — —

Norman Hold on, I'll get someone for you to speak to.
Jenkins Yes, why don't you do that.
Norman I think you'd better wait in the porch.
Jenkins Oh, all right.

Jenkins steps back out of the door and Norman closes it as —

  Eric enters from the bedroom, slipping on his jacket

Norman Eric, there's a gentleman waiting outside.
Eric Norman, I'm trying to get to the station.

Eric opens the front door

Norman He's from the Department of Social Security.

Eric slams the front door on Jenkins

Eric I beg your pardon?
Norman And he wants to see a Mr Thompson.
Eric What?
Norman A DSS Inspector is here to see a Mr Rupert Thompson. I said that there must be some sort of a mistake — —
Eric (*urgently*) What exactly did you tell him?
Norman Just that I'd get him someone to talk to.

Eric starts to move Norman UR *to the stairs*

Eric Good thinking, Norman. I'll see to him.
Norman (*stops and realizes*) Wait a minute!

Eric What?

Norman He means Mr Thompson — your *old* lodger.

Eric (*trying to appear offhand, stopping him*) No. No, he doesn't.

Norman Yes. Rupert Thompson. You know, the gentleman who had the upstairs before me.

Eric No. No, he doesn't mean him.

Norman Yes, he emigrated to Canada. They keep on delivering his mail here.

Eric I know that, Norman.

Norman Yes. You have to send it on to him. All his social security bits and pieces.

Eric No, it's not that Mr Thompson he wants to see.

Norman Yes, it must be. I'll go and tell him — —

Eric No!

Norman — that Mr Thompson emigrated years ago.

Eric No! You mustn't!

Norman Why not?

Eric Because *I'm* Rupert Thompson.

Norman Well, I can still tell him that he — — (*Then realizing*) *You're* Rupert Thompson?

Eric I'm *pretending* to be Rupert Thompson.

Norman tries to work this out, but — —

Norman No, no, you've lost me.

Eric opens the front door and smiles at Jenkins

Eric (*to Jenkins*) Won't keep you a moment.

As Jenkins goes to answer, Eric closes the door on him. Eric pulls Norman aside

(*To Norman*) Can you keep a secret, Norman?

Norman (*worried*) A secret? I think so.

Eric Ever since Mr Thompson left here two years ago — I've been cashing in his social security benefits.

Norman To send on to him, you mean.

Eric Not quite. No.

Norman Well, to send back to the DSS then?

Eric Not quite. No.

Norman Well then what do you do with all ... (*Realizing*) Oh, my God!

Eric (*urgently*) Shush!

Norman That is disgraceful!
Eric I know.
Norman How could you, Eric?
Eric It's a long story and now's not the time. Just keep out of the way and
I'll deal with it. It won't be anything serious.

Jenkins pokes his face in through the letter box

Jenkins (*calling*) Hallo!
Eric (*calling*) Won't be a moment!

Jenkins lets the letter box close

Eric pushes Norman away from the front door, towards the kitchen

(*To Norman*) Now get in there and keep quiet — and don't listen at the
door.
Norman Why? You have told me everything, haven't you, Eric?
Eric (*lying, with a broad smile*) Norman!

*Eric pushes Norman into the kitchen, slams the door, then rushes to the front
door and calls*

(*Calling*) Coming!

Then he stops, suddenly remembering something

(*To himself*) Mr Thompson? Ah! Gout! Mr Thompson, gout.

*Eric throws his jacket into the window-seat, then dives to the umbrella stand,
grabs a short umbrella, realizes his mistake and grabs a walking stick and
hobbles quickly to open the front door*

(*To Jenkins*) Sorry for keeping you. (*Indicates his leg*) I don't get about that
well, I'm afraid. Do come in.
Jenkins Thank you.

*Jenkins enters the living-room. Throughout, Eric hobbles about, as if his leg
is very painful*

Mr Rupert Thompson?
Eric (*glances at the kitchen, then back*) Er, yes. Rupert Thompson at your
service. What can I do for you, Mr, er — —
Jenkins Jenkins.

Mr Jenkins.

Jenkins George Jenkins, Department of Social Security, Sickness and Disability Division.

Eric (*worried*) Sickness and Disability Division, I see. This has got nothing to do with the phone call earlier?

Jenkins No.

Eric Ah. (*Then, trying to be pleasant*) Would you like to sit down?

Jenkins That would be very nice, thank you.

Eric leads Jenkins DC *where he sits on the sofa and takes out a thin file*

I won't waste your time, Mr Thompson. I just have a couple of points, then I'll be out of your hair.

Eric Good. Well, fire away.

Jenkins (*referring to papers in the thin file*) Mr Thompson, according to our records, you have been laid up in bed for the past six months with gout.

Eric (*pained*) Yes, that's right, severe gout. Caused by complications resulting from a crate falling upon my foot during unpaid voluntary employment packing food for famine relief — I have all the doctor's reports upstairs.

Jenkins (*indicating the thin file*) I have copies of them here.

Eric Oh yes?

Jenkins (*indicating the thin file*) As well as all your benefit claims.

Eric (*worried now*) Oh yes?

Jenkins Yes. In fact, I happen to have copies of the entire household's medical reports and social security claims with me.

Jenkins reaches into his briefcase and takes out a huge thick folder, overflowing with bulging multi-coloured papers and reports

Eric Will you look at that.

Jenkins I must say, 344 Chilton Road is a very unlucky household.

Eric Isn't it just?

Jenkins Almost jinxed.

Eric That's a very big folder you have there, Mr Jenkins.

Jenkins Largest in the Borough.

Eric (*laughing*) You're boasting again.

Jenkins doesn't get the joke

Jenkins There's everything in here, Mr Thompson. Retirement pensions, family benefits, child care, single parent benefits, sick pay, housing benefit and invalid care.

Eric (*thinking that's the end of the list*) And all under this one roof.

Jenkins Guardian's allowance, widow's allowance, maternity pay, National Health refunds, redundancy payments and several industrial injuries benefits.

Eric (*again thinking that's the end*) Who'd have believed it?

Jenkins Christmas bonuses, vacation bonuses, cold weather compensation and miscellaneous disease benefits.

Eric Goodness.

Jenkins And free milk. Yes, if it wasn't for all the confirmatory medical and legal backup documentation, we might think there was something funny going on.

Eric Would you?

Jenkins Oh, Mr Thompson, you'd be amazed at what some people do get up to — false claims, fake bank accounts, phoney names.

Eric Nooo!

Jenkins Forged prescriptions, fake IDs.

Eric Noooo!

Jenkins Multiple claims for a single disability.

Eric That's a good one — I mean, it's good that one can spot these things.

Jenkins Isn't it just. (*He fishes in his briefcase and takes out several forms*) Now, as I was saying, I have this form for you to sign.

Eric (*unsure*) You do?

Jenkins Just to confirm that you've been receiving our sickness benefit for the last six months.

Eric Er — that's right.

Jenkins And as there are no signs of improvement — —

Eric Er — that's right.

Jenkins — you are therefore now due to receive our Industrial Injuries Disablement Benefit.

Eric (*not expecting this*) I'm what?

Jenkins (*checking his notes*) That's an extra weekly income of — er — twenty-four pounds and ninety-three pence.

Eric Oh, no, really, the unemployment benefit is plenty for me.

Jenkins But you're eligible, aren't you, sir?

Jenkins offers Eric a pen with the form. Eric's not sure what to do. Reluctantly he signs. Jenkins takes it back and signs as well. Eric looks concerned

Now, I am just signing as a witness to your signature, Mr Thompson. It all seems to be in order.

Eric Oh, good. Well, if that's everything then.

Eric stands Jenkins up. Jenkins sits again

Jenkins Almost. I'll just need your Mr Swan's signature then I'll be on my
way.

Eric I beg your pardon.

Jenkins Mr Swan. Your landlord.

Eric What about him?

Jenkins I will need his signature to confirm that you have indeed been
convalescing here for the past six months.

Eric (*really friendly*) Oh, you don't need that.

Jenkins (*friendly, right back at him*) Oh, yes, I do.

Eric Ah, well, I'm afraid he's not in.

Jenkins At work, is he?

Eric That's right. He's at work. Hard at work at the Electricity Board. (*He
stands Jenkins*) So why don't you leave all this with me and I'll get Mr
Swan to sign everything then send it all back to you in the post.

Jenkins (*sitting*) You're forgetting departmental regulations.

Eric Am I?

Jenkins I have to be present when Mr Swan signs.

Eric Do you?

Jenkins To witness his signature as I witnessed yours just now.

Eric (*standing Jenkins again*) Well, if you come back later, I'm sure he will
have come home.

Jenkins Mr Thompson, I think I should tell you that I'm under strict orders
from my superior, our *Ms* Cowper.

Eric *Ms* Cowper?

Jenkins Yes. Our *Ms* Cowper gave me explicit instructions to sort out this
matter before I leave this residence.

Eric Is that so?

Jenkins And you wouldn't want to get the wrong side of our *Ms* Cowper,
let me tell you.

Eric No, I'm sure. (*He gets Jenkins up*) I'll tell you what, if you'd like to set
yourself up in the dining-room, I'll see if I can find someone — *him* — Mr
Swan, that is — at work — to come home and sign your forms for you.

Jenkins Oh, very well.

Eric You'll be happier in there. You can spread yourself out on the dining-
room table.

*Eric ushers Jenkins into the dining-room, gently closes the door and rushes
to the kitchen*

Jenkins re-enters and Eric quickly returns to his pained hobble

Jenkins Oh, Mr Thompson!

Eric Yes?

Jenkins If you have a moment, I wouldn't say no to a cup of tea.
Eric Of course, Mr Jenkins.
Jenkins Earl Grey, if you have it.
Eric Of course.

Jenkins exits into the dining-room, Eric pulls open the kitchen door

Norman!

Norman, who has been listening at the keyhole on his knees, falls in. Eric quickly pulls him to his feet

Get up.
Norman Oh, my God! I feel worse than I did before.
Eric Pull yourself together.
Norman I think I'm going to be sick.
Eric We haven't got time for that.
Norman You said there wasn't any more I should know about.
Eric Shh!
Norman I heard everything, Eric.
Eric Shhh!
Norman All those claims!
Eric Shhhh!
Norman What happened to just cashing in Mr Thompson's cheques?
Eric It all got a bit carried away.
Norman I'll say!
Eric Well, they kept on offering me all this money. I never asked for it.
Norman What?
Eric All right, here's the story. Two years ago the Electricity Board got
  privatized and handed out their special Christmas bonuses. That's thirty
  per cent redundancies. I'm out of a job. I can't bring myself to tell Linda,
  and then, out of the blue, Mr Thompson's cheque arrives and saves the day.
  I think, "Great, I'll find work in January." Well, the New Year arrives and
  there's no work, no money. However, the DSS sent all these forms from
  their various divisions.
Norman Divisions?
Eric One division asked me if I had any other lodgers living here so I made
  up a couple of names and said — "yes" — and they sent me some money.
  Then somebody else asked me if they were all employed and I said — "no"
  — and they sent me some more money. Then somebody else asked me if
  everybody was healthy and I said — "no" — and they sent me even more
  money. And somebody else asked me if there were any pensioners living
  here and I said ...

Norman I get the picture!

Eric Well, before I knew what I was doing, everything had snowballed.

Norman Snowballed, it bloody avalanched!

Eric Shush!

Norman What you've done is a very serious offence.

Eric I know.

Norman You could go to jail.

Eric I know.

Norman What did you do it for?

Eric Twenty-five thousand a year and no tax.

Norman Bloody hell!

Eric Shush!

Norman But you're going to go to prison, Eric.

Eric No, I'm not.

Norman Yes, you are. How can you sign as Mr Swan, when he thinks you're "hop-a-long" Thompson?

Norman imitates Eric walking with a limp

Eric Stop that! The solution is simple. Someone has got to pretend to be me.

Norman What?

Eric (*straight at Norman*) Pretend to be me — —

Norman Pretend to be you?

Eric — and sign the forms for Mr Jenkins.

Norman Come off it. What idiot are you going to get to do that?

Eric puts his arm around Norman. Norman realizes

Oooh. No, I couldn't. (*He pulls away*) I won't.

Eric You must.

Norman No. I refuse to participate in such a dishonest scheme. Get Linda to sign.

Eric Linda?

Norman She's the landlord here as well as you.

Eric No, Norman, Linda can't sign.

Norman Why not?

Eric Because she doesn't know what I've been doing. She thinks I still work for the Electricity Board.

Norman Bloody hell! Does anybody know what you're up to?

Eric Only my Uncle George.

Norman (*amazed*) Your Uncle George — you mean that sweet old man who cleans up at the local hospital?

Eric That's right.

Norman Well, how on earth did he find out?

Eric He didn't find out. He's my partner.

Norman Partner?

Eric Shush! Well, after I'd told the Sickness and Disability Division that a few of my made-up lodgers were ill, they suddenly wanted to see all their medical documentation — prescriptions and the like — I knew I'd be in trouble if I couldn't show them anything, so I asked Uncle George and he helped me out by getting all the medical forms I needed from the hospital.

Norman I can't believe I'm hearing this. I've got to go in there (*he indicates the dining-room*) and tell that Mr Jenkins the whole story.

Eric (*stopping him*) No! You can't do that!

Norman It's my duty.

Eric You can't!

Norman Give me one good reason why I can't!

Eric You're not here.

Norman (*stops, then confused*) Not here?

Eric That's right. You're at a funeral.

Norman (*confused*) A funeral?

Eric Yes.

Norman Whose funeral?

Eric Yours.

Norman (*beat*) Mine?

Eric That's right — You died this morning.

Norman tries to work this out

Norman (*shakes his head*) No, no. You've lost me again.

Eric I have to tell you something.

Norman (*wary*) Should I sit down for this one?

Eric You might want to *lie* down.

They sit on the sofa. Eric tries to smile broadly

I've been using your name as part of my fiddle.

Norman (*standing, furious*) My name?

Eric (*pulling him back down*) Shush!

Norman What do you mean, "my name"?

Eric The DSS thinks that Norman Bassett has been living upstairs for the past two years.

Norman Well, I have been.

Eric As an unemployed lumberjack.

Norman What?

Eric With a wife and family to support.

Norman Wife and family?

Eric It's cramped, but you're happy.

Norman Why on earth a lumberjack?

Eric Well, you had to be out of work.

Norman So?

Eric Well, there's not much call for lumberjacks down the Mile End Road, is there?

Norman God! And I died this morning?

Eric Look, I could see the whole thing was out of control. I had to find a way out, Norman. I thought, "I know, I'll kill off all my made-up characters, one by one."

Norman Well, that sounds like a good idea.

Eric So I rang the DSS this morning and told them that Norman Bassett the lumberjack had died.

Norman Great.

Eric Not great. Now they're going to send a funeral re-imbursement, a widow's payment, widowed mother's allowance and extra child care!

Norman Oh, my God!

Eric I'd already tried emigrating your brother to Australia — they sent me a relocation fee. I put your father in jail — "boom", criminal severance pay. I sent your sister off to Africa to become a missionary and it's like I've won the bloody lottery. I can't get rid of anybody! I'm stuck in a nightmare, Norman — I want to get out, but they keep giving me more and more money!

Norman Bloody hell!

Eric (*suddenly realizing*) Norman, you have to help me. If that Mr Jenkins starts an investigation with the police, your name is bound to come up and no-one will believe we weren't in partnership.

Norman Partnership?

Eric (*again realizing*) Oh, God, worse than the police — There's your fiancée.

Norman (*worried*) Brenda?

Eric She'll be devastated. Your wedding might have to be postponed.

Norman Postponed!

Eric If not cancelled.

Norman Cancelled!

Eric (*begging*) You have to help me.

Norman (*angrily*) Do you know what you are?

Eric Up until now — bloody lucky.

Norman You're insane.

Eric If you don't help me, Norman, I could be dead by dinner time.

Norman (*angrily*) You might not make it to dinner time!

Eric turns for the dining-room, when the kitchen door opens and —

Uncle George, a chirpy old man, enters, wearing a hospital porter's uniform

George Morning all!

Eric Uncle George!

George Morning, Eric, my boy. Came in the back way, hope you don't mind. (*He steps towards Norman*) Morning, Norman.

Norman (*sternly*) *Et tu, Brute*?

George Beg pardon?

Eric Nothing. Norman's a bit upset.

George Yeah, I'd be upset 'n' all if I was getting married on Saturday.

Eric hurries to George to usher him back into the kitchen

Eric Not now, Uncle.

George Norman, did I ever tell you about the time I almost married Ivy Parsons the coalman's daughter ...

Eric We know, you got cold feet.

George No, cold feet was the other one — Rosie Clark. God — Rosie Clark! No, Ivy caught me in the back seat of her Austin Seven with her sister — God, you should have heard her language — —

Eric Come back later, Uncle George.

George (*turning back into the room*) Oh, all right. Here, you know your washing machine's still making that funny noise?

Eric It doesn't matter. (*To George*) Norman's got a little problem.

Norman (*angry*) Ha!

George Worried about your nuptials, are you, lad? Wehay!

Eric There's been a death in the family, hasn't there, Norman?

Norman Yes. And another one coming up fast.

George Oh dear. Well, you have my commiserations, my old son. Was it someone close?

Norman Yes, very!

Eric Yes. It's very sad. (*Quickly, taking George aside*) And I'm dealing with a visit from the Department.

George What?

Eric Sickness and Disability Division.

George Ooooh!

Eric They're in the dining-room.

George (*checking his watch*) Blimey, well, I can't stay long. I just popped over to tell you that I might have a bloke interested in the assorted National Health wigs.

Norman Wigs?

Eric Fine.

George But still not so much as a nibble at the support corsets.

Norman Corsets?

Eric Well, I've stashed them up in the back of the top cupboard when you need them.

George Top cupboard, right.

Norman Corsets and wigs?

Eric All right, all right — It's just the other part of what I've been up to.

Norman Other part?

George 'Ere, 'ere, don't give the game away.

Eric It's OK. Norman's part of the set-up now.

Norman Norman's no such thing.

Eric Look, all the free stuff the Health Service sends me, Uncle George flogs down the car boot sales. There's maternity dresses.

George Maternity bras.

Eric Alopecia wigs.

George Surgical stockings.

Eric Support corsets.

Norman No wonder the Health Service is going broke!

Eric Now, off you go, Uncle George.

Eric pushes George to the front door and turns back for the kitchen. Norman follows

George I'll see you at the church on Saturday, Norman.

Norman Oh, God, the church — Eric, if Brenda finds out ...

Eric Just go and introduce yourself to Mr Jenkins as me and I'll fix his tea.

Eric exits into the kitchen

Norman glances at the dining-room then hurries after Eric

Norman I'll fix his sugar.

Norman exits into the kitchen as —

George opens the front door to reveal Sally Chessington, a young welfare worker, in the doorway, just about to knock

Sally Good-morning.

George Good-morning.

Sally I've called about poor Mr Bassett.

George Poor Mr Bassett?

Sally (*sympathetically*) Yes, I'm from the local family crisis department.

George Oh, yes?

Sally Yes, Mr Swan telephoned the DSS earlier this morning and informed them of Mr Bassett's passing.

George Passing what?

Sally Passing away. Apparently Mr Swan indicated that the Bassett family was very distressed.

George Did he?

Sally Yes, so the DSS immediately sent word to my superiors, who thought someone should be sent round to help out.

George But Mr Bassett's in the kitchen, making a cup of tea.

Sally (*confused*) Mr Bassett's making a cup of tea?

George That's right.

Sally (*realizing*) Oh, you must mean his son.

George Whose son?

Sally Poor Mr Bassett's son, of course. Is he very upset?

George He is a bit, there's been a death in the family.

Sally Yes, I know. That's why I'm here. Mr Bassett's father has died.

George His dad? Oh, he said it was someone close.

Eric pushes Norman out through the kitchen door; neither notice Sally. Eric carries the tray of tea and Jaffa Cakes

Eric Just wait here and I'll fetch him from the dining-room.

Norman Couldn't we just say that Mr Swan has left the country or something?

Eric No!

George (*to Sally*) This is Mr Bassett now. (*Then, to Norman*) I'll see you on Saturday then?

Norman (*over his shoulder*) Yes, at the church, Uncle George.

George And I'm sorry about the news you've had.

Norman Not half as sorry as I am.

George exits

Norman performs a couple of practice "Hello's"

Sally My sincerest commiserations, Mr Bassett.

Norman turns at the unexpected voice

Norman Commiserations?

Sally I'm here from the phone call earlier.

Norman What phone call?

Sally We spoke to a Mr Swan.

Norman Oh, yes. The phone call. Commiserations to Mrs Bassett.

Sally Yes, that's right. It's a terrible loss.

Norman Oh, yes, it's a shame. It would have been lovely.

Sally (*confused*) What would have been lovely?

Norman An ocean cruise for their golden wedding anniversary.

Sally Golden wedding anniversary?

Norman In a couple of months from now.

Sally Oh, dear.

Norman (*leading her back to the front door*) Well, it's very nice of you to pop over but I'm afraid I'm a bit busy right now.

Sally I won't get in the way.

Norman But you might, Miss ... ?

Sally Chessington — Sally Chessington — you must be so very sad.

Norman Well, as Mum always says, you have to look on the bright side.

Sally The bright side?

Norman At least we ended up with the toaster.

Sally A toaster?

Norman It's not bad.

Sally A toaster? (*Getting angry*) I think it's terrible that a man can work so hard and yet all his family ends up with is a toaster.

Norman It's only a raffle.

Sally A raffle?

Norman Either you win or you don't. It's the luck of the draw. Fate wasn't shining on my mum and dad this morning.

Sally Goodness. I must say, you're taking it all very well.

Norman Thank you.

Sally And I'm sure he's resting peacefully now.

Norman Who?

Sally Your father.

Norman considers this and checks his watch

Norman No, I doubt that.

Sally You do?

Norman Yes. He'll be at that allotment by now.

Sally Allotment? (*Then understanding*) Oh, I see. *The* allotment. The great allotment in the sky.

Norman I beg your pardon?

Sally Now that he's passed away.

Norman Now that who's passed away?

Sally Why, your father, of course.

Norman My father?

Sally (*confused*) Yes.
Norman Passed away?
Sally (*confused*) This morning.

Norman suddenly breaks down in tears and sits. Sally sits by him

Norman Oh, God!
Sally That's all right, Mr Bassett.
Norman We were gonna go fishing in the morning!
Sally I bet Norman loved his fishing.
Norman I'm sorry, but this is such a shock, I mean I only spoke to him on the phone last night, he said, "Don't forget your worms, Son!" (*He sobs again, then he realizes*) "Norman"?
Sally Dear departed Norman.
Norman Dear departed Norman?
Sally I'm sure you'll miss your father.
Norman My dear departed father, Norman.
Sally Yes.
Norman Norman the *lumberjack*.
Sally Yes.

Norman considers this

Norman So, you're not from the Women's Institute?
Sally No, Mr Bassett, I'm from the council's family crisis department.
Norman Oh, you've come to the right place.

Norman jumps up to explain but the dining-room door opens and —

Eric enters, ushering Jenkins in. Jenkins has a cup of tea in one hand and a Jaffa Cake on a plate in the other

Eric If you'd just like to come through now.
Jenkins Thank you, Mr Thompson.
Eric And *Mr Swan* will be happy to answer all your questions.
Norman (*rushing to meet them*) No!

Sally is soon at Norman's side

Eric And here he is now.
Norman Mr Thompson, if I could just — —
Eric Later — leave the introductions to me.
Norman (*to Eric, indicating Sally*) You don't understand.

Eric Later!

Jenkins (*a little confused*) But, we met at the door.

Eric (*to Jenkins, indicating Norman*) You did indeed, Mr Jenkins, I'd like you to say hallo to Mr Swan.

Norman (*smiling at both Sally and Jenkins*) Yes, I'd *also like* you to say hallo to Mr Swan — but you can't.

Jenkins Can't?

Eric Can't?

Norman No. Eric's not at home.

Jenkins (*confused, to Eric*) But you just told me in there that Mr Swan had come back for early elevenses.

Eric (*pleasantly to Jenkins*) Yes — (*then angrily to Norman*) — he had.

Norman Yes. Mr Swan was here, but now he's gone.

Eric Gone?

Jenkins Gone?

Norman Yes, He had his elevenses, then he left.

Eric Had his elevenses?

Jenkins That quick?

Norman Yes. He just blew in here, ate some baked beans and blew out again.

Jenkins (*to Eric*) Mr Thompson, you should have impressed upon Mr Swan the urgency of the situation.

Eric (*pleasantly to Jenkins*) Yes — (*then angrily to Norman*) I realize that!

Sally (*standing at Norman's back*) Is there anything else I can do for you, Mr Bassett?

Eric (*irritated*) Bassett? You — —

Norman No, I'm fine, thank you, Sally. Oh, this is Sally. Sally, this is Mr Jenkins and Mr Thompson. Sally just popped in, she'll be popping out again in a moment.

Jenkins Bassett, Bassett — Wait a minute. That name rings a bell.

Norman (*worried*) Does it?

Jenkins Yes, "Bassett". You're another of Mr Swan's resident lodgers, aren't you?

Norman Er — that's right.

Jenkins Yes. Bassett — family of six.

Norman (*angrily*) Six?

Jenkins Three children, the grandmother and Mr and Mrs Bassett themselves.

Eric Yes, the Bassetts. There's all sorts up there.

Sally barges next to Jenkins

Sally Sir, I don't know who you are but you are being most indelicate to Mr Bassett.

Jenkins (*unsure*) Indelicate?

Norman steps in between them

Norman That's all right, Sally.
Eric Excuse me — —
Sally You shouldn't let him talk to you like that, Mr Bassett. Not today.
Jenkins Oh?
Norman I can handle it.
Eric Excuse me — —
Sally (*putting her arm around Norman*) This man needs care, support and
   sympathy.
Jenkins Why, what's happened?
Sally His father passed away this morning.
Jenkins Oh, tragic.
Norman Oh, bloody hell.
Eric What's going on, Norman?
Norman (*quickly*) Norman — ly! Normally. Normally, I would have said
   something earlier, but I forgot.
Eric Forgot what?
Norman I forgot that my father dropped down dead this morning.
Eric (*concerned*) Did he?
Norman Yes. And we'll all miss my father "*Norman*", won't we, Mr
   Thompson?
Eric (*understanding*) Oh. *Your* father "Norman" — —
Eric   ⎱ (*together*) — Yes, we'll all miss him.
Norman ⎰
Norman Say "goodbye", Sally.
Jenkins You say your father passed away this morning?
Norman That's right.
Jenkins So you're Norman Bassett's son?
Norman Yes.
Jenkins (*fishing*) Which makes you?
Norman (*hopefully*) Very sad?
Jenkins Your name.
Norman Oh, I see. Mr Bassett.

*Not good enough for Jenkins, so behind Jenkins' back, Eric indicates a little
boy*

   Er — junior.

Still not good enough, so Eric sticks up two fingers behind Jenkins

The second.
Jenkins Your first name?
Norman Oh, it's — —

Norman looks to Eric for help

Eric ⎫ (*together*) ⎧ Er — John.
Norman ⎭   ⎩ Er — Thomas.
Eric ⎫ (*together*) ⎧ Er — Thomas.
Norman ⎭   ⎩ Er — John.
Jenkins Well, which is it, John or Thomas?
Eric Well, it's — er, both, isn't it, John-Thomas?
Norman Yes.
Jenkins John-Thomas? (*Checking his notes*) But according to the Bassett family file, Norman's eldest son is called William Richard.
Norman That's right. William Richard. When I was at school everyone teased me and called me Willie-Dickie, now everyone just calls me — John-Thomas.
Jenkins Willie-Dickie, John-Thomas. I don't get it.
Eric It doesn't matter, Mr Jenkins.
Jenkins (*to Sally*) Willie-Dickie, do you get it, miss?
Sally Oh, yes, I get it.
Norman Yes, she gets it, he gets it and I get it. Willie-Dickie, that's me.
Jenkins But I still don't understand — according to our records, Norman Bassett's eldest son, William Richard — —
Norman That's me.
Jenkins — is stone deaf.
Eric (*remembering*) Ah.
Sally Deaf?

Everyone turns to face Norman — who cups a hand to his ear

Norman (*feigning acute deafness*) I'm sorry, I missed that one.
Jenkins He's been receiving our criminal injuries compensation for the last eighteen months.
Norman I've what ... ? (*Then feigning deafness*) — did you say again?
Eric (*trying to lighten it*) Yes, poor Willie has been stone deaf since the place where he worked was held up.
Sally (*not understanding*) The place was held up and Willie went deaf?
Eric They blew up the safe and burst both his ear drums.
Sally (*to Norman, still standing at his back*) But you've understood every word that I've said.

Norman says nothing, looking the other way, busily examining his finger-nails

Eric (*clearly to Norman, indicating Sally*) Your friend's talking to you, Willie.

Eric turns Norman's head to face Sally

(*To Sally*) You have to look right at him when you talk to him.

Eric turns Norman's head back to him

(*To Norman*) Willie reads lips. Don't you, Willie?

Norman looks back at Sally

Norman Yes — by Braille.

From now on, Sally and Jenkins speak loudly and clearly when addressing Norman. Sally pulls Norman's face to her whenever she speaks to him

Sally (*to Norman*) I had no idea.
Eric It's a burden he's learnt to live with, Sally. (*To Norman, pulling his face*) Haven't you, Willie?
Norman (*looks back at Sally*) I suppose I have, yes.
Jenkins Yes, but I hope the unemployment benefits have helped to ease the grief.
Norman (*tersely, to Eric*) Unemployment benefits?
Eric (*trying to lighten it, nodding to Norman's head*) Yes.
Sally Unemployed as well.
Eric Yes. Poor Willie has been trying to find work for the past year. (*To Norman*) Haven't you, Willie?
Norman I suppose I have, yes.
Eric But it's all been to no avail. (*He shakes Norman's head*) Not even a whisper of a job.
Jenkins No. Particularly as he was such a specialist before the accident.
Norman Specialist?
Jenkins Well, I wouldn't suppose there's much of a call for deaf piano tuners, is there?
Eric No.
Norman (*angry*) Piano tuner?
Sally (*turning Norman's head to her*) You poor man. Your entire livelihood destroyed by a meaningless act of violence.
Norman (*vaguely*) Yes ...

Eric (*escorting Sally away*) Listen, Sally, it was very nice of you to pop round and make sure Willie was all right.

Sally Well, when you've got something to give — —

Eric But as you can see, he's coping just fine.

Sally But, I'm sure there must be something I can do.

Eric Thank you, there's nothing, is there, Willie?

Norman No, you've done enough already, Sally.

Sally But there's all the funeral arrangements to be seen to.

Norman The what?

Sally (*very loud and clear*) The *funeral arrangements*. (*Brightly*) Why don't *I* handle all that for you?

Norman Ooooh, no.

Sally You just tell me if it's to be a cremation or burial.

Norman It doesn't matter!

Sally What?

Norman I don't care!

Eric Steady, Willie!

Jenkins Goodness me. Have some respect for your poor dead father.

Eric (*stepping in, to Sally*) You must forgive Willie. He's upset. (*Then, to Norman*) Aren't you?

Norman Yes. Very.

Sally Willie, your father must have left some last wishes?

Norman I think he wanted to be pushed off the end of Brighton pier.

Jenkins Good heavens!

Eric (*quickly*) No, no, no. (*He hobbles to Jenkins*) What Willie meant was that Norman wanted a burial at sea. (*He hobbles to Sally*) Now, why don't we let Sally go off and see what she can work out for us and we'll talk to her later. All right?

Sally Yes. You leave everything to me, Mr Thompson. (*She smiles at Norman*) Keep it up, Willie-Dickie.

Norman Thank you, Sally.

Sally exits through the front door

Eric Well, that's got that settled. (*To Jenkins*) Now, where were we?

Jenkins Mr Swan.

Eric (*nonchalantly crossing back*) Yes?

Norman stamps on Eric's foot and Eric immediately returns to his limping

I mean, "Yes, Mr Swan" — you missed him. I know what — if you give me your address, I'll tell Mr Swan to stop off at your office on his way to work tomorrow.

Jenkins Mr Thompson, I should remain here until this matter is settled. Remember our Ms Cowper.
Eric How could I forget. You have another cup of tea and I'll see if he's got back to work yet.
Jenkins Good. I want this matter settled with Mr Swan as soon as possible.
Eric Of course. Help yourself to another Jaffa Cake.

Jenkins exits into the dining-room. Eric shuts the door behind him

Norman What have you done?
Eric Don't panic — all we need is another Swan to sign — we're just back at stage one.
Norman Stage one! (*Indicating the dining-room*) He thinks you're a lame-legged lodger called Thompson (*indicating front door*) and she thinks I'm an out-of-work, recently bereaved deaf piano tuner with a dickie willy!

Uncle George opens the kitchen door and enters with a cardboard box

George Eric, my boy!
Eric Later, Uncle George. Our situation hasn't improved.
George Sorry to hear that, but I'm afraid I've got some returns for you, Eric.
Norman Returns?
Eric Now's not the time, Uncle.
George It's these surgical stockings. (*He takes a pair of baggy, blue, woollen stockings out of the box and waggles them in the air*) They're just not moving.
Eric Oh, no. I've got a suitcase full of them up in the cupboard.
Norman A suitcase full of stockings?
Eric Surgical stockings, Norman. NHS standard varicose vein issue.
George They were our hottest selling line last Christmas. I think it's the colour, Eric. Autumnal pastels are in this season.

Eric takes the box from George and nudges him back towards the kitchen door

Eric This really isn't the time, Uncle George.
George I just need to take those wigs from the cupboard.
Norman (*trying to usher George out*) Not now, Mr Swan.
George But I need the wigs ——
Norman Come back later, Mr Swan.
Eric (*realizing*) Mr Swan!
George Yes?
Eric (*indicates Uncle George*) Mr Swan!

Norman Oh, no!
Eric It's perfect.
Norman It's preposterous! It would never work.
George What would never work?

Eric pulls George aside

Eric (*indicating all named in the speech*) Uncle George — that inspector
needs a Mr Swan's signature. Now, I can't sign Swan because he thinks I'm
Thompson and Norman can't sign Swan because he thinks he's his own
son whose father's passed on and Linda can't sign Swan because she
doesn't know what's going on. So, we need you to sign Swan — but not
as "you" Swan, as "me" Swan, so we've got a Swan to sign "Swan" — —

George considers this and turns to Norman

George Sounds logical to me.
Eric Excellent! (*Indicating George's porter's uniform*) We'll have to get
him a change of clothes.
George You could just tell it was an odd job day and I've been working about
the house.
Eric No, you're meant to have been at work — at the Electricity Board,
remember.
George Electricity Board, right.
Eric Everything I've got will be too big for him — what about you, Norman?
Norman I'm not going to help you any further, Eric.
Eric You must. Remember your Brenda — left alone when her fiancé was
carted off to prison where he spent ten years for conspiring to defraud Her
Majesty's Government.
Norman I think I've got something upstairs that might fit him.
Eric That's the spirit! We'll dress you in the bedroom, Uncle George. Just
go and get your clothes, Norman!
George Hey, Norman — this is living!
Norman Living!

Eric exits into the bedroom DR *with George as* — —

Linda Swan enters through the front door

Norman passes Linda. Throughout, Linda seems terribly upset by something

(*Without a concern*) Morning, Mrs Swan.
Linda Norman?

Norman disappears up the stairs for a beat, then comes crashing back down — stops dead

Norman Mrs Swan. You're in the living-room.
Linda I realize that, Norman. So are you.
Norman You're not meant to be in the living-room.
Linda Neither are you, Norman. You're supposed to be at work.
Norman So are you, Linda.
Linda Never mind me. I'd be grateful if you left me alone.
Norman That's not a good idea.
Linda I'm expecting a visitor.
Norman A visitor?
Linda Yes. And it's private.
Norman But it might not be.
Linda It is!
Norman Eric didn't say anything about a private visitor.
Linda Eric doesn't know. Now please go back upstairs.
Norman Mrs Swan, I really don't think you should be having private visitors that Eric doesn't know about — —

Linda bursts into tears

Mrs Swan ...?
Linda Just leave me alone!

She moves to the bedroom door

Norman (*quickly stepping in between Linda and the bedroom door*) No!
Linda What now?
Norman You're not allowed in there, Mrs Swan.
Linda What are you talking about. Let me into my bedroom!
Norman No, you can't. It's not allowed.
Linda Not allowed? Who said so?
Norman The — er — Health Department. Yes, I had to call them in because of the smell.
Linda From my bedroom?
Norman Yes! It was this terrible, yucky smell — what a pong! The Health Department has put your bedroom into quarantine.
Linda Quarantine?
Norman Apparently, it's an outbreak of some horrible virulent, contagious disease — "Blurr!".
Linda In my bedroom?
Norman Yes.

Linda That's awful.

Norman It's *bloody* awful. The Health Department has been here spraying all morning. That's why you can't go into the bedroom — (*suddenly realizing*) or the dining-room.

Linda The dining-room, as well?

Norman locks the dining-room door and pockets the key

Norman Yes, it spread. You're going to have to sleep with me.

Linda I beg your pardon?

Norman You'll feel better.

Linda Sleeping with you?

Norman I mean upstairs — in my flat — tonight — with Eric. When he comes home from work — from the Electricity Board — where he works.

Jenkins bangs on the dining-room door

Linda What's that?

Norman (*feeling for rain*) Thunder.

Linda There's someone in the dining-room.

Norman No, no. I don't think so.

Jenkins (*off, calling*) Hallo, I think I've been shut in!

Linda Who's that?

Norman (*to Linda*) Oh, that. That's nobody. (*Then, calling through the door*) Don't worry. Everything's under control! (*Then, to Linda*) It's a gentleman from the Health Department.

Linda A gentleman from the Health Department?

Norman Yes. They left him behind.

Jenkins (*off, calling*) I think the door's stuck!

Norman (*calling through the door*) I'll be with you in a minute!

Jenkins (*off, calling*) Is that Mr Bassett?

Norman (*calling through the door*) Yes.

Jenkins The Mr Bassett I was talking to earlier?

Norman That's right.

Jenkins (*off, calling*) Then how can you hear me?

Norman considers this and looks blankly at Linda

Norman (*loudly through the keyhole*) I beg your pardon?

The phone rings and Linda answers it immediately

Linda (*on the phone*) Hallo, Swans' residence? ... Brenda?

Norman Oooh, Brenda! Please let me talk to her.
Linda (*on the phone*) Brenda, he can't talk right now. ... What? No, I don't
know why he didn't go to work. ... No! Don't come over here!
Norman (*grabbing the phone*) No, please don't ...
Linda Shut up, Norman! (*Grabbing the phone back*) He'll see you
tomorrow.

She goes to hang up, then goes back to the phone

(*On the phone*) Brenda, I know we've never met, but I promise you, I'm
not always this rude. Look, I'll see you on Saturday at the church, all right?
Goodbye.

Linda hangs up

Norman Is she all right?
Linda She was worried about you.
Norman I know how she feels.
Linda Norman, I'm going to make myself a cup of tea — and you'd better
be out of my living-room by the time it's brewed.

Linda exits into the kitchen and Norman calls after her

Norman Then make sure it's good and strong.

*Norman slams the kitchen door shut on Linda. He locks the door and the
phone rings*

(*On the phone*) Hallo, Brenda! ...

Jenkins bangs on the dining-room door

Jenkins (*off, calling*) Open this door!
Norman (*on the phone*) Goodbye, Brenda!

Norman hangs up the phone and starts towards the dining-room

(*Calling*) Coming!

Eric enters from the bedroom DL

Eric Where are those clothes for Uncle George?
Norman Oh, thank heavens!

Eric Haven't you got them yet?
Norman Disaster!
Eric What? No clothes?

Jenkins bangs on the dining-room door again

Jenkins Please let me out!
Eric What's the matter with Mr Jenkins?
Norman (*holding up the key*) I locked him in the dining-room.
Eric Why?
Norman It seemed like a good idea at the time!

Eric snatches the key from Norman and starts to unlock the dining-room door

No!
Eric Be quiet, Norman.
Norman (*indicating the kitchen door*) But you don't understand. In the kitchen ...
Eric Shut up, Norman.

Eric opens the dining-room door to reveal Jenkins

I'm sorry, these old door frames are sticking all the time.

Jenkins steps into the living-room, carrying a plate of Jaffa Cakes

Jenkins (*to Eric*) Mr Thompson, it is nearly ten o'clock.
Eric I know.
Jenkins If Mr Swan isn't here, I must contact our Ms Cowper. May I use your telephone?
Eric No!
Jenkins What now?

Eric hobbles to Jenkins

Eric Mr Swan is here.
Jenkins Is he?
Eric Yes. He came back.
Jenkins Well, can I see him?
Eric Er — no. He's not ready yet.
Jenkins Not ready? Well, where is he?
Eric He's — er — on the roof.
Norman Oh, my God.

Jenkins On the roof?

Eric Yes.

Jenkins What's your landlord doing up on the roof in this weather?

Eric Fixing up the new satellite.

Jenkins But he was at work ten minutes ago.

Eric Yes, he suddenly remembered.

Jenkins This is all very odd.

Eric And that's what he remembered, it's odd job day. He came back from work and went straight up on to the roof. He'll be down in three minutes.

Linda bangs on the kitchen door

Jenkins Who's that?

Norman looks about pretending he heard nothing

Norman Who's what?

Jenkins Someone's banging.

Norman (*shocked*) At this time of day?

Jenkins On that door. (*He points behind Norman to the kitchen*)

Norman Oh, yes?

Jenkins (*to Eric*) Well, who is it, Mr Thompson?

Eric (*lost*) Well, who is it, Willie?

Norman It's — er — my mother.

Eric Your mother?

Norman Yes.

Jenkins You mean Mrs Bassett?

Norman (*reluctantly*) Yes.

Jenkins Your widowed mother?

Norman (*even more reluctantly*) Yes. My widowed mother.

Linda (*off, calling*) This door's been locked!

Eric (*realizing it's Linda, rushing to the kitchen door*) Hagh! (*He turns back to Jenkins and makes exactly the same sound*) Hagh! (*Then, slowly changes the shocked sound to a sad one*) "Ah", ah, aaah — the poor bereaved woman.

He takes Norman aside

What's she doing here ... ?

Jenkins Mr Bassett, why has your widowed mother been locked in the kitchen?

Norman Well, we had to. She heard the news about Daddy passing away and she went berserk.

Jenkins Good heavens, perhaps someone should let her — —
Norman No! No, you have to remember that it's that time of year, as well.
Jenkins That time of year?
Norman Her moon is in Uranus.
Jenkins It's where?
Eric Astrologically speaking. Willie's mother goes quite funny at this time of year and that combined with the bereavement ...
Norman Yes, she's been tearing up the carpet, eating the wallpaper in the kitchen ...
Jenkins Eating the wallpaper?
Eric Yes. This is for her own good. I know, why don't we go up to the attic?
Jenkins The attic?
Eric Yes, we can climb out on to the roof from there and sort out this business right away with Mr Swan.
Norman That's a good idea. I'll go first.
Eric (*urgently*) No, Willie, you should stay down here and deal with your mother.
Linda (*off, with very loud banging and shouting*) Let me in!
Jenkins Don't you think you should let that poor woman out?
Eric Oh, no. No, that's not a good idea, is it, Willie?
Norman Oooh, no, we've just had new wallpaper in here.
Eric Now, Mr Jenkins, to the attic — we can sort out this business right away.
Jenkins Oh, very well. Let me grab my files.
Eric You grab whatever you need.

Jenkins exits into the dining-room UL

Eric quickly takes Norman aside

Right, you've got five minutes maximum. When we get back from the roof I want Uncle George dressed up as me in one of your suits.
Norman What about Linda?
Eric Just keep her locked up.

The phone rings and Norman picks it up

Norman (*on the phone*) Hallo? ... Oh, thank goodness, Brenda.

Jenkins enters from the dining-room with his heavy, bulging files

Jenkins Right then, Mr Thompson.

Jenkins walks into Norman on the telephone and they both stop — then —

(*To Eric*) What on earth is Willie doing on the telephone?

Norman (*as if he can't hear anything*) Hallo? Hallo, is there anybody there? Hallo?

He hangs up

(*To Eric*) Would you believe it? There's nobody there again.

Eric (*explaining to Jenkins*) Poor Willie's never quite got the hang of telephones since the accident. Have you, Willie?

Norman Just gone half-past.

Eric Is it really? We'd best be off then, Mr Jenkins.

Jenkins Well, I just have one question concerning Mr Bassett's hearing.

Eric It's very sad, isn't it?

Jenkins I dare say, but I was just talking to him and he understood every word I said.

Eric I told you, Willie reads lips.

Jenkins Through solid oak doors.

Eric Yes, he's got very keen eyesight.

Before Jenkins is able to consider this, Eric pulls him out through the UR *stairs arch*

The phone rings and Norman picks it up

Norman (*on the phone*) Hallo, Brenda!

Linda (*off, calling*) Norman!

Norman (*on the phone*) Goodbye, Brenda!

Norman hangs up and backs to the UR *arch*

No! The gentleman from the Health Department said that you have to stay in the kitchen until further notice!

Norman exits through the UR *arch*

Linda (*off, calling and banging*) Open up!

The front door opens and Dr Chapman, a mild-mannered marriage guidance councillor enters

Dr Chapman (*quietly*) Hallo?

Linda (*off, calling*) Is there anybody there?

Dr Chapman (*looking about; quietly*) Only me.

Dr Chapman gently rests his head against the door, listening

(*Softly*) Hallo?
Linda (*off, suddenly calling as she bangs loudly*) Unlock this door!
Dr Chapman Oh!

Dr Chapman quickly unlocks the door and —

Linda storms in, tea in hand

Linda (*furious*) Norman, if you don't stop playing silly buggers! (*Then, great relief*) Oh, Dr Chapman.
Dr Chapman Mrs Swan, are you all right, Mrs Swan?
Linda No, I'm not!
Dr Chapman Would you like to sit down?
Linda (*yelling up the stairs*) Stupid idiot, Norman!
Dr Chapman Let's take a few deep breaths. (*He does*)
Linda What with him mucking about and having to meet you this morning.
Dr Chapman That's all right.
Linda I've been very anxious about it, you know.
Dr Chapman I can see that — —
Linda Dr Chapman, I never thought I'd have to talk to anyone about my husband.
Dr Chapman I can understand — —
Linda Let alone a marriage guidance counsellor — —
Dr Chapman Relationship arbitrator — —
Linda And Norman Bassett, our upstairs lodger, hasn't helped.
Dr Chapman Hasn't he?
Linda (*shouting up the stairs*) He's been a bloody nuisance!

Dr Chapman takes a note of this

Dr Chapman Has he? Well, you approached your local council for help. And that's why I'm here.
Linda Thank you, Dr Chapman. (*Calming herself*) Would you like a cup of tea, I've just made one.
Dr Chapman In a moment, perhaps.
Linda You know, I think I'd rather just get on with it as well — show it to you. Get it all out in the open.
Dr Chapman However you would like this to go, is just perfect. Questioning a partner's sexuality is never an easy task.
Linda No. It's over here.

During the following, Dr Chapman follows Linda L *as she arranges the chair to step up to the cupboard*

I found it all by complete accident tucked away at the back of the cupboard, when I was looking for our old 8mm cine films. I was going to have them transferred to video for our anniversary.

Dr Chapman holds the chair for her as she clambers up, opens the high cupboard, delves deep and take out a large cardboard box

This is it. Prepare yourself for a shock, Doctor Chapman.
Dr Chapman This is precisely what your local council has trained me for, Mrs Swan.

Linda takes out a long blonde wig from the box, holds it up, then passes it down to Dr Chapman

Linda This is the first thing I found.
Dr Chapman (*trying to remain unstirred*) I see.
Linda (*then handing him a lady's corset*) Then this —(*then a floral maternity dress*) and this —

Dr Chapman holds the dress against himself

(*Taking out a pair of stockings and handing them to Doctor Chapman*) — and these — and this.

She takes out a large maternity bra from the box and hands it down to Dr Chapman

He is astonished

It's amazing, isn't it?
Dr Chapman Well, your husband's certainly got himself well organized, Mrs Swan. Tell me, Eric's mother ...
Linda Yes?
Dr Chapman Is she a blonde, by any chance?
Linda Well, yes.
Dr Chapman (*examining the large bra*) And is she a big woman?
Linda Well, largish — does that mean anything, Doctor?
Dr Chapman Well, I think I'm beginning to see a pattern emerging here. Could be the result of a Suppressed Mother Fixation.
Linda Oh, God.

Dr Chapman Luckily it's early days and this fetish is still very personal to your husband.

Linda (*upset*) His fetish?

Dr Chapman Yes. I don't imagine Eric will have yet gained the confidence to venture out and about.

Linda (*more upset*) Out and about?

Dr Chapman I doubt if he's going that wild. I imagine Eric just likes to slip into his favourite frock and parade up and down in front of the bedroom mirror.

Linda (*even more upset*) In front of the bedroom mirror!

Dr Chapman You mustn't distress yourself, Mrs Swan.

Linda But you're telling me my husband's "gay"!

Dr Chapman No, no, no. Not all cross-dressers are — that way inclined.

Linda Cross-dresser!

Dr Chapman Now, I'm not saying that your husband doesn't have a problem — (*he glances at the size of the maternity bra*) — a large problem — but — —

Linda A large problem!

Linda turns and runs for the kitchen

Dr Chapman Mrs Swan! Don't alarm yourself!

Linda exits into the kitchen, slamming the door behind her as —

George enters from the bedroom, wearing long underwear and his porter's hat

George Am I going to get dressed up or what?

Dr Chapman turns to see George in his state of undress

Dr Chapman Goodness!

George Oh.

Dr Chapman And who exactly are you?

George Wait a minute — are you the gentleman from the local authorities?

Dr Chapman That's right.

George Oh, sorry. (*He crosses to shake Dr Chapman's hand*) Yes, well, Swan's the name.

Dr Chapman Gracious me. You mean you're Mr Swan?

George Yes.

Dr Chapman (*he glances at the kitchen*) Mr *Eric* Swan?

George Oh, yes, yes, I am Eric Swan. Eric Swan, that's me. So, shall we get on with it?

Dr Chapman I beg your pardon?

George You want me to sign a statement or something, don't you?

Dr Chapman Well, I thought we might start with a bit of a chat.

George A chat?

Dr Chapman Yes.

George Oh, all right then. What shall we chat about?

Dr Chapman I suppose I had just better be straightforward and honest about it, hadn't I?

George (*a little lost*) Honesty is always the best policy, as my lovely dear mother used to say.

Dr Chapman Ah, your lovely dear mother. (*He makes a note of this*) Well, I know all about it.

George All about what?

Dr Chapman What you've been indulging in — on the quiet.

George (*worried*) What do you mean?

Dr Chapman I've seen your get-up in the cupboard.

Dr Chapman shows George the open box of clothes

George Not what was in the box?

Dr Chapman I'm afraid so. Yes.

George God, I didn't think you were here to chat about that.

Dr Chapman Yes. I'm afraid it's all come out into the open.

George About what's been going on here.

Dr Chapman That's right.

George You mean you've come here to make an arrest.

Dr Chapman Mr Swan, there's no question of an arrest.

George Well, I have to make something perfectly clear to you, I am not who — — (*realizing*) No question of an arrest?

Dr Chapman That's right.

George Why not?

Dr Chapman Well, it's not illegal, is it?

George (*brightly*) Isn't it?

Dr Chapman No.

George You mean that what I've been doing with the wigs and the stockings and the dresses isn't against the law.

Dr Chapman That's right.

George (*happily*) Blimey! Well, then I'd have thought that everybody would've been at it!

Dr Chapman I'm not sure about that, Eric — You don't mind if I call you "Eric"?

George Oh no, you call me "Eric".

Dr Chapman Well, I don't think it's highly approved of, Eric. But certainly a lot of people do do it.

George Do they?

Dr Chapman It's a free country.

George It certainly is! I only wish I'd found out earlier that it was legal.

Dr Chapman Oh yes?

George I'd have got the whole family at it!

Dr Chapman I must admit, Mr Swan, this isn't quite the reaction that I had expected.

George And I can tell you, my partner will be very relieved as well.

Dr Chapman Your partner?

George Yes.

Dr Chapman Are you saying that there's somebody else who — er— indulges in this with you?

George That's right.

Dr Chapman Would it be too impolite of me to ask who?

George You're sure it's legal?

Dr Chapman Quite sure, Eric.

George Well then, it's my Uncle George.

Dr Chapman Your Uncle?

During the following, George crosses, puts the clothes back in the box and the box back in the cupboard

George (*proudly*) Actually, the clothes were all Uncle George's idea.

Dr Chapman Were they?!

George I thought we should just stick to the wigs, but clever old Uncle George insisted that we got into dresses and corsets.

Dr Chapman Did he?!

George (*full of himself*) Oh, yes, Uncle George. He's the one who really knows the tricks of the trade.

Dr Chapman (*he writes in his notebook*) Does he?

George Oh, yeah ...

Linda suddenly bursts out of the kitchen in a rage

There is a loud bang as the door crashes into George who remains hidden US *of the open door through the following speech. Linda stands in the doorway*

Linda Dr Chapman! I'm going round to Eric's office and have it out with him!

Dr Chapman Mrs Swan!
Linda Make him confess to everything!
Dr Chapman Your husband's here, Mrs Swan.
Linda We've been married ten years! (*Then realizing what Dr Chapman just said, all her bravado fades away*) Eric's here?
Dr Chapman Yes.

Linda goes to speak, bursts into tears and runs back into the kitchen, slamming the door

Mrs Swan!

Dr Chapman is about to rush into the kitchen when George emerges from behind the door on very unsteady legs. Dr Chapman has to steady him

Are you all right, Mr Swan?

George can only just stand

Goodness. Do you often have comeovers like this?
George (*dazed*) The door, the door.

George weaves from side to side, holding his head and Dr Chapman hurries to him with a chair, seating him quickly, still in a direct line with the door

Dr Chapman There you go. I'll get you something to drink.

George flops forward, his head sinking down in front of his knees

Linda bursts back out of the kitchen, hitting him again

Linda Dr Chapman!
Dr Chapman Mrs Swan, I ...
Linda Where is my husband?
Dr Chapman Mrs Swan, prepare yourself for a shock.
Linda What?
Dr Chapman There's somebody else involved with your husband's cross-dressing.
Linda What?
Dr Chapman I'm afraid it's true.
Linda God, who?
Dr Chapman Eric's Uncle George.
Linda Uncle George?

Dr Chapman Yes, and from what Eric's told me, it's Uncle George who's
been leading your husband astray.

Linda I can't believe it. Eric and Uncle George.

Dr Chapman Yes, and Eric indicated that they've been indulging in it for
several years.

Linda (*bursting into tears again*) Of course! His Uncle George used to take
him camping!

Dr Chapman Mrs Swan!

*She runs back into the kitchen, this time Dr Chapman follows her through
the kitchen door closing it to reveal George slumped in his chair*

*Mustering all of his weary and wobbly strength, George manages to stand,
placing the chair to one side. Without warning —*

*Linda crashes back out of the kitchen, crashing the door into George once
more —*

She runs across the stage, exiting into the bedroom

*Dr Chapman hurries out of the kitchen after Linda, crashing the door into
George once more*

Mrs Swan!

Dr Chapman exits into the bedroom as —

*Norman enters through the stair's archway with a bundle of clothes and
moves towards the bedroom door*

Norman Uncle George, come on out.

George stumbles out from behind the kitchen door

George (*foolishly*) Hallo.

Norman dashes across to George, just as he faints into his arms

Norman Oh, my God!

Norman starts to drag George back to the sofa as —

Sally and Mr Forbright enter through the front door. Forbright is dressed

*in a dark suit. They are both horrified at what Norman is doing. This can
look quite rude as Norman tries to pull George up from behind*

(*To the unconscious George*) Up we come.
Sally Mr Bassett!
Norman Agh!

Norman falls on the sofa in fright with George

Sally, I thought I'd got rid of you.
Sally Willie, I've brought Mr Forbright.
Norman Sally, please —
Sally Mr Forbright is an undertaker.
Norman Well, that's all very well, but — (*then realizing and worried*)
Undertaker?
Sally Yes. He's here to take care of everything.
Norman Oh, bloody hell.
Forbright Mr Bassett, whatever are you doing?
Norman Doing?
Forbright You shouldn't be trying to move the body on your own.
Norman Body?
Forbright Yes. (*Indicating George*) Your dear departed father, "Norman".

Norman looks quickly to George

Norman (*thinking madly*) Ah — er *that* body. (*Then, crying*) I'm so
confused. Dear Daddy. Norman Bassett.

Sally notices it's George

Sally Wait a minute, when I arrived earlier this morning, you said that this
man was Uncle George.
Norman (*thinking madly*) Ah, no, no, that was somebody completely
different. Uncle George has gone now.
Sally But he looks the same.

Norman peers very closely at George

Norman He does, doesn't he?
Sally Practically identical.
Norman That's right, they're twins.
Sally Twins?
Norman Uncle George is dear Daddy's twin brother.

Sally Goodness, well, Uncle George must be shattered.
Norman He's knocked out.
Sally Willie, I think you should leave everything to Mr Forbright.
Norman I'd much prefer to do everything myself, honestly. It's no trouble
at all. I can borrow a spade, dig a bit of a hole —— —
Forbright Willie, is there a bedroom we could use on this floor?
Norman Bedroom?
Forbright I just need somewhere for your father to rest peacefully.

Norman leads them to the dining-room

Norman No, all the bedrooms are being used. Sally will show you the way
through here. You can lay him out on the dining-room table.
Sally The dining-room table?
Norman Yes, we'll eat out tonight.

*Norman pushes Sally off and Forbright stops in the dining-room doorway,
turning to Norman*

Forbright Your father's in a better place now.
Norman Yes. (*He nods sympathetically and shuts the door on Forbright*)
And I wish I was with him. (*He hurries back to George*) I'll get you some
smelling salts, Uncle George!

Norman hurries into the kitchen as —— —

Eric enters from the UR *archway*

Eric (*calling up the stairs*) I don't know how I could have got it wrong, Mr
Jenkins, I could have sworn that's where Mr Swan went to.
Jenkins (*off, calling*) It's all right.
Eric (*calling up the stairs*) And I had no idea how dusty it was up there.

*Jenkins enters down the stairs, covered in dust. He has removed his jacket
and his shirt is blackened with filth — he doesn't have his briefcase or files
with him*

Jenkins I'm sure it'll come out after a couple of washes.
Eric I do apologize, Mr Jenkins. (*Then with mock surprise, seeing George
resting up on the sofa*) Wait a moment — here he is now.

Eric leads Jenkins to the back of the sofa

Jenkins So this is your elusive Mr Swan.
Eric Yes, this is my landlord. Mr Swan, say hallo to Mr Jenkins.

George doesn't move

   *Forbright enters unnoticed from the dining-room and walks up quietly
   behind them both*

Jenkins Is he deaf as well?
Eric No. Nothing like that.
Jenkins Well, what's the matter with him, then?
Forbright He's dead.

Eric looks in amazement at Jenkins and —— —

—— the CURTAIN *falls*

ACT II

The action is continuous

Jenkins, Eric and Forbright stand behind the sofa on which lies the unconscious George. Eric looks back at Forbright

Eric
Jenkins } (*together*) Dead?

Forbright (*nodding solemnly*) Yes, dead I'm afraid. This poor gentleman slipped away from us earlier this morning.

Eric Slipped away?

Jenkins Mr Thompson, did your landlord fall off the roof?

Eric I'm not sure what's happened, actually.

Forbright I'm told it was very peaceful.

Eric Well, that is a relief.

Forbright covers George with the blanket Norman used in Act I as — —

Norman hurries back in from the kitchen, carrying a large half-filled rubbish bag. He doesn't see Forbright

Norman I couldn't find any smelling salts, (*indicating the rubbish bag*). But this is enough to bring anyone round, Uncle George.

Forbright What is that, Mr Bassett?

Norman (*realizing the undertaker has returned*) I was just saying that the bin men are coming round — by George!

Forbright Mr Bassett, I was looking for a cloth for the dining-room table.

Eric A cloth for the ... (*He limps across to Norman*) What on earth has happened down here, Willie?

Norman Nothing. Nothing at all.

Forbright I'm preparing to lay out the body on the dining-room table.

Eric Lay him out?

Forbright (*indicating Norman and George*) Yes, this young man's father has died.

Norman Oh, God.

Jenkins (*to Eric*) Willie Bassett's father? I don't understand, Mr Thompson.

Eric Join the club.

Norman takes Forbright's arm and leads him towards the dining-room

Norman Yes, thank you, Mr Forbright. You'll find a table-cloth in the far chest. And there's knives and forks in the dresser if you need them.

He pushes Forbright into the dining-room and closes the door

Well, there we are then.
Jenkins Willie Bassett's father? (*To Eric, indicating George*) But you just told me that this was your landlord, Eric Swan.
Eric That's right, I did. And it is.
Jenkins How could Mr Swan have been Willie Bassett's father?

Eric draws a blank, turns to Norman and smiles broadly

Eric You explained that to me once, didn't you, Willie?

Norman just looks straight at Eric

Norman (*feigning deafness again*) I'm sorry, Mr Thompson, did you say something?
Jenkins Mr Bassett!
Eric That's you, Willie.
Jenkins (*loudly "mouthing" deaf for Willie Bassett*) How could Mr Swan have been your father?
Norman (*caught*) Well — when I was a little boy, my father, (*angrily to Eric*), the lumberjack, (*then pleasantly to Jenkins again*) lost his job. The family fell upon hard times and so they decided — to have me fostered here with Mr and Mrs Swan.
Jenkins So Mr Swan was your foster father.
Eric Yes, on his mother's side.
Jenkins (*to Norman*) Are you saying that both your natural father *and* your foster father passed away this morning?

Norman glares at Eric

Norman Yes.
Eric Yes. Mr Eric Swan here (*he indicates George*) and Mr Norman Bassett — er — upstairs (*he indicates upstairs*).
Jenkins You've lost two fathers in one day.
Norman Yes.
Eric Yes, he's very careless.
Jenkins Goodness me. And how did your real father, Norman Bassett the lumberjack, how did he die?

Norman He fell out of a tree.

Jenkins Good God, and his body's upstairs?

Norman Yes, that's where he landed.

Jenkins And is the undertaker dealing with that body as well?

Eric No, that's a surprise for later. And obviously, Mr Swan won't be able to sign your forms, Mr Jenkins. So I think it best if we just forget about my claim for increased benefit.

Norman (*happily*) That's very generous of you, Mr Thompson.

Eric A small sacrifice, considering your losses, Willie.

Eric opens the front door for Jenkins and smiles confidently

Yes, I'm sorry, Mr Jenkins, but you'll have to return to your office empty-handed.

Jenkins (*happily helpful*) Oh, but I won't.

Eric Won't you?

Mrs Jenkins Not at all. *Mrs* Swan can sign your forms.

Norman Oh, God.

Norman sits on the chair L, his head down in his hands

Eric I beg your pardon?

Jenkins I think we'll find, Mr Thompson, that according to your lease, *Mrs* Swan is your landlord as well as the late Mr Swan.

Eric Is she?

Jenkins Yes. And if that's the case, then it would be perfectly in order for Mrs Swan to confirm that you have been convalescing here, from your gout, for the past six months.

Eric (*very worried*) Oh, that is good news.

Jenkins So is she home?

Eric No. No, she's definitely not home. She's at work.

Dr Chapman enters from the bedroom

Dr Chapman Oh, sorry to interrupt.

Eric is motionless. Drawing a blank, he looks at Jenkins, draws another blank. Eric looks back to Dr Chapman

Eric You're new around here, aren't you?

Dr Chapman I am actually, yes. Has anyone seen Mr Swan?

Eric and Jenkins glance down at the covered unconscious George

Eric No. No, Eric's — er — no longer with us. (*Warily*) And — er — who wants to know?

Dr Chapman I'm Dr Chapman.

Eric (*worried*) Doctor?

Dr Chapman Yes. I suppose Mr Swan's resting.

Eric Resting?

Dr Chapman Yes. He was hit by a door.

Jenkins (*to Norman*) Good heavens, is that how it happened then?

Norman just stuffs a piece of cake in his mouth

Linda enters from the bedroom

Linda Have you found him yet, Dr Chapman? (*She sees Eric and holds back her emotions*) Oh.

Eric (*caught, to Linda*) Ah — now, I know who you are.

Linda And I'm beginning to know who *you* are — Dr Chapman and I need to talk to you in private.

Eric, still limping, takes Linda to one side

Eric (*happily*) We have company.

Linda I don't care if the Queen Mum popped over for — (*realizing*) Why are you limping?

Eric I wasn't limping.

Linda You've got a walking stick.

Eric Oh, that, yes. It's nothing. It's just playing me up again.

Linda What is?

Eric My old, you know, in the leg.

Linda What are you talking about?

Jenkins It's his gout.

Eric Yes, thank you, Mr Jenkins.

Linda Gout?

Eric Oh, yes, and it's very sore.

Linda (*to Eric*) You haven't got gout.

Jenkins What?

Eric (*full of energy*) Yes, that's what I like! Positive thinking. Positive thinking! Mind over matter. You are so right! I must keep telling myself I haven't got gout! I haven't got gout! I — (*Suddenly, he experiences a "miracle healing" and performs a jig in celebration*) God! Look at that! I feel better already. Marvellous, thank you.

Dr Chapman Maybe I should come back at a more convenient moment.

Norman looks up from his despair

Norman I think we should all come back at a more convenient moment.

Linda crosses to Norman and Dr Chapman sits on the edge of the sofa

Linda I told you to push off upstairs.
Jenkins I believe he's involved down here, actually.

Linda steps up to Jenkins

Linda And who are you?

Norman jumps up between Linda and Jenkins

Norman Oh — he's fine.
Linda What?
Norman You asked, "How are you?". And he's perfectly well. Wasn't feeling too good earlier on, but now he's just fine. (*Then, to Jenkins*) Aren't you?
Jenkins Yes.
Linda Norman!
Norman (*interrupting*) Normal! Normal, yes, he's absolutely normal now.
Linda I asked "Who" he was!
Norman (*to Eric*) Ah, she said, "Who".
Eric (*to Linda*) It sounded awfully like "How" to me as well.
Linda Shut up! (*Then, to Jenkins*) Who are you?
Jenkins I'm — —

Norman jumps between Linda and Jenkins again

Norman (*interrupting*) The gentleman from the dining-room.
Linda What?
Norman This is the gentleman that was stuck in the dining-room. (*To Jenkins*) Aren't you?
Jenkins Yes.
Eric There we are then.
Jenkins And who are you, madam?
Norman Oh, she's fine as well.
Jenkins (*for deaf Willie Bassett*) I asked "Who" she was!
Eric ⎫ (*to each other*) Oh, he said, "Who".
Norman ⎭
Jenkins (*to Linda*) Who are you?

Linda I'm — —

Norman jumps back between Linda and Jenkins

Norman (*interrupting*) The lady from the kitchen!
Jenkins (*very worried, backing away*) Not the wallpaper lady?
Norman That's right! This is the lady that was stuck in the kitchen. (*To Linda*) Aren't you?
Linda (*tersely*) Yes.
Eric (*happily*) Yes, the gentleman from the dining-room and the lady from the kitchen. Well, I think that's enough introductions for one day, how about a nice pot of tea?

Eric tries to pull Linda to the kitchen

Linda I just made a pot of tea!
Eric Well, make a fresh one.
Dr Chapman (*standing*) I wouldn't mind putting the kettle on.
Linda (*firmly*) Sit down.
Dr Chapman (*sitting*) Certainly.
Jenkins (*to Linda*) You say you're the lady from the kitchen?
Linda That's right.
Jenkins (*to Linda, indicating Norman*) You mean you're his — —
Norman (*interrupting*) Yes. That's right.
Eric Yes, she is.
Jenkins But she looks so young.
Linda What?
Norman Doesn't she? What a nice thing to say. (*To Linda*) Did you hear that? That is so sweet of Mr Jenkins, saying how young you look — that Oil of Ulay's obviously doing the trick, isn't it?
Eric It certainly is.
Norman Why don't you go and put a mud pack on right away.

Norman tries to push Linda away

Linda Get off me.
Jenkins Mr Bassett — —
Norman Yes, that's me.
Jenkins (*indicating Linda*) Are you saying that this is the widow?
Linda The widow?

Norman shakes his head and points at the window

Norman (*baby talk*) No, that's the widow over there.

Jenkins What?

Norman Yes, that's the lickle widow, (*indicates the door*) and that's the lickle dwoor, (*points up*) and that's the lickle ceiwing up dere.

Jenkins (*shouting*) I said — Oh, never mind. (*He turns to Linda*) Is he saying that you are his — —

Eric (*interrupting*) Yes. That's exactly what he's saying.

Linda (*to Eric*) His what?

Norman (*to Linda, foolish baby talk*) Woo are my lickle cuddly-mummy-bunny, aren't woo?

Linda What?

Norman I know lickle woo is all upset and teary-dropping about lickle Daddy going to heaven, but pwease don't take it out on lickle me.

Linda Why are you talking like that?

Norman (*pushing Linda closer to the kitchen*) Just put the kettle on.

Linda I'm not making any tea!

Norman Please make some tea. (*Then, for Jenkins' benefit*) Like woo did in the old days.

Linda Old days?

Norman When you used to pick me up from school.

Linda (*to Eric*) What is he talking about?

Eric indicates that he has no idea

Norman Woo always used to have a cup of tea and a slice of cake ready for me to do my homework.

Linda Get out! I just want to talk to my husband!

Jenkins (*astonished, glancing upstairs*) Talk to your husband?

Eric Yes! (*Then sympathetically for Jenkins' benefit*) Yes, I'm sure you do.

Linda What?

Eric (*solemnly*) Yes. I'm sure you would like to be able to talk to your husband. We all would. (*To Norman*) Wouldn't we?

Norman (*even more solemnly*) Yes. But we can't.

Linda Can't?

Norman (*tearful*) No. A few last words would be wonderful, but alas.

Linda What are you talking about, Norman?

Norman Yes! (*Crying, for Jenkins' benefit*) "Poor Norman", that's exactly who I'm talking about. Now what about that tea?

Linda I said I don't want any tea!

Dr Chapman (*standing*) I really wouldn't mind putting the kettle on.

Linda (*tersely*) Sit down.

Dr Chapman Certainly.

Linda (*to Eric*) Will you please get rid of Norman!

Jenkins (*staggered, glancing upstairs*) Get rid of Norman?

Eric Don't you think we should just "let him be" for a while?

Linda No.

Jenkins (*astonished*) "Get rid of Norman"? How can you talk like that, madam?

Linda Very easily.

Eric Oh, he's OK here.

Norman Yes, he's OK.

Linda (*to Jenkins*) I'm sick of him hanging around the house like a bad smell.

Jenkins Good God!

Eric Please, he's very peaceful where he is.

Norman Very peaceful.

Linda (*to Eric*) Look, if you don't do it, I'll throw him out into the street!

Jenkins Madam, have you no respect?

Linda What for?

Jenkins (*clasping his hands in reverence*) Well, for poor Norman?

Linda Not today, no.

Jenkins Especially today, madam.

Linda He's being more of a bloody nuisance today than usual.

Jenkins I beg your pardon?

Linda I'm having a terrible day and all he can do is lie about the house looking stupid.

Jenkins I've never heard anything like it in my life.

Linda (*indicating upstairs*) I wish he'd just bugger off up there where he belongs.

Jenkins Good God!

Eric Mr Bassett, why don't you take Mr Jenkins into the kitchen and make him another cup of tea.

Jenkins I've had enough tea to sink a battleship!

Norman How about a wee mid-morning sherry then?

Dr Chapman (*getting up*) I think I could use a small sherry.

Norman ⎫
            ⎬ (*together to Dr Chapman*) Sit down.
Jenkins ⎭

Dr Chapman (*sitting*) Certainly.

Jenkins I think it's a little early for sherry, Mr Bassett.

Norman No, it's all right, the clocks have just gone back.

Jenkins Oh.

Norman Follow me.

Jenkins Oh, and in the meantime, perhaps you could locate Mrs Swan for me.

Norman pulls Jenkins off into the kitchen and Eric slams the door on them

Linda Locate "Mrs Swan"?

Eric Never mind that.

Linda (*to Eric, indicating the kitchen*) Why is that man looking for me?

Eric (*to Linda*) He's not looking for you. (*He indicates Dr Chapman*) And why is *this* man looking for *me*?

Linda (*to Eric*) He *is* looking for me.

Dr Chapman (*to Eric*) I'm not looking for you.

Eric (*to Dr Chapman*) You just asked for "Mr Swan".

Linda (*to Eric, indicating the kitchen*) And he just asked for "Mrs Swan".

Dr Chapman (*to Eric*) But you're not the Mr Swan that I want.

Eric (*to Linda, indicating the kitchen*) And you're not the Mrs Swan that *he* wants. He's looking for my mother.

Linda (*to Eric*) Your mother?

Eric (*to Linda*) That's right.

Dr Chapman (*to Eric*) Ah, so your name's Swan as well then?

Linda ⎱ (*together to Dr Chapman*) Yes!
Eric ⎰

Dr Chapman (*sitting and writing*) Aha!

Linda (*indicating the kitchen*) That is the gentleman from the Health Department?

Eric Er — yes.

Linda The one who's been spraying the bedroom for that contagious disease?

Eric Er — yes.

Linda So what does he want with your mother?

Eric She needs to be fumigated.

Linda Fumigated?

Linda breaks R and stands L of the sofa which still has the unconscious George covered with the blanket

Who's that?

Eric (*trying to steer her away*) That? That's nobody.

In one deft movement, Linda whips off the blanket like a magician to reveal the semi-dressed George

(*Hopefully*) Abracadabra?

Dr Chapman Heavens, it's Mr Swan.

Linda What the hell's happened to him?

Eric He's OK. He was hit by a door.

Linda He's in his underwear.

Dr Chapman (*standing*) He was in his underwear when I arrived.

Eric Yes, he was, wasn't he?

Linda (*now worried*) Why for God's sake?

Eric Well — er — he was in the middle of getting changed.

Dr Chapman Changed?

Eric Yes.

Linda Into what?

Eric He wanted to borrow something of mine.

Linda Something of yours!

Eric Yes. He likes to get all dressed up from time to time.

Linda All dressed up! How could you do this to me?

Eric Do what?

Linda Think what it must feel like to find out?

Eric (*still utterly lost*) Find out?

Linda You're a transvestite!

Eric tries several times to answer, but draws a blank each time. He is totally confused and lost

Dr Chapman (*thinking he's worked out who Eric is*) So this must be Uncle George.

Linda turns back to Dr Chapman, who is sitting by Uncle George

Linda Of course it's Uncle George!

Dr Chapman Good.

Linda (*to Eric*) How can you be so blatant about this?

Eric Blatant?

Linda I might have guessed something like this was going to happen when you gave up smoking.

Eric Smoking?

Dr Chapman Mrs Swan, I don't think you can blame your husband's condition on the fact that Uncle George gave up smoking.

Linda Uncle George never smoked.

Dr Chapman Then how could he give it up?

Linda (*to Eric*) My God, you even used to play rugby!

Dr Chapman Or on Uncle George giving up rugby.

Linda Uncle George never played rugby!

Dr Chapman (*to Eric*) Are you sure your name's Swan?

Eric ⎱ (*together*) Yes!
Linda ⎰

Dr Chapman sits, even more confused

Sally enters from the dining-room and Eric rushes to her

Sally I think we're ready for — Oh, where's young Mr Bassett?
Eric He left and you can leave too.
Sally But I'm still busy.
Dr Chapman Does Uncle George have any brothers?
Linda No.
Sally Well, he used to have a twin brother, Norman.

Eric gives her an angry look

Dr Chapman Ah.
Linda Twin brother?
Eric (*to Sally*) Yes, thank you, you can leave now.
Dr Chapman Was it Uncle Norman who used to smoke and play rugby?

Everyone looks at Dr Chapman

Excuse me.

Dr Chapman hurries off into the bedroom

Eric (*to Sally*) Now will you please go.
Sally But I'm still engaged.
Eric It doesn't matter.
Linda Engaged?
Sally Yes, Mr Bassett.

Behind Sally's back, Eric indicates his wedding ring enthusiastically

Eric Yes, engaged, Mr Bassett.

For an instant, Linda is delighted to meet who she believes is Norman's fiancée

Linda Oh, you must be — (*remembering her earlier phone call*) Oh God, the phone call earlier — —
Sally Yes.
Linda — I'm sorry if you thought I was rude.
Sally Rude?
Eric Rude? No, she didn't think you were rude.
Linda (*still upset, but delighted, taking Sally's hands*) Well, it's wonderful to meet you at last.

Sally I beg your pardon?
Linda This is a lovely surprise.
Sally Surprise?
Linda I didn't think I'd get to see you until Saturday.
Sally Saturday?
Linda At the church.
Sally Church?
Eric (*miming*) Yes, the church. Here's the church, here's the steeple, look
    inside there's all the people.

Linda pulls Eric aside

Sally Oh, the church. On Saturday. (*Then, trying to be as delicate as possible*)
    The date's been fixed then?

A moment as Linda absorbs this

Linda (*unsure towards Sally*) Yes.
Sally Oh, I don't think I'll be able to be there for that.
Linda I beg your pardon?
Sally I've already made other plans.
Linda Other plans?

Linda shares an anxious glance with Eric. Eric shrugs

    What about Norman?
Sally What about the poor man?
Linda If you don't turn up on Saturday, he'll be devastated.
Sally Who will?
Linda Norman, of course.
Sally (*tries to fathom this, but ...*) Norman's dead.
Linda What?
Eric What a thing to say!
Sally Well, he is.
Eric Oh, so that's how it is, is it?
Sally That's how what is?
Eric "He's dead". Just like that. Love 'em and leave 'em flat, ay?
Sally What?
Linda I couldn't agree more. That's very cold.
Sally What is?
Eric One moment you love him to the end of the earth, then the next moment,
    it's "Oh, he's dead" and you just dump him like an old sack of potatoes!
Sally What are you talking about?

Eric You've probably got a new boyfriend already.
Sally Mr Thompson!
Eric And that's his name, is it?

Eric takes Sally by the arm and leads her back to the dining-room door as — —

Dr Chapman appears from the bedroom

Dr Chapman I've completed my notes and I'd like to arrange another meeting for some other time.
Linda I want this sorted out today!
Eric (*to Sally*) You get back in there and consider your position.
Sally Consider my what?
Eric Just get in there and shut up.

Eric slams the dining-room door on her

Linda What an awful woman!
Eric Isn't she?
Linda Get rid of her! Get rid of everybody! Dr Chapman and I want to talk to you alone!
Eric Do you?
Dr Chapman Do we?
Linda Yes — about your mother!
Eric You want to talk about my mother?
Dr Chapman Uncle George's mother?
Linda (*furious, indicating Eric*) *His* mother!
Eric You want to talk about my mother?
Linda (*bursting into tears*) Yes — and what big boobs she's got!

Linda runs into the bedroom

Dr Chapman starts to say something important, then changes his mind

Dr Chapman Excuse me.

Dr Chapman exits into the bedroom as — —

Eric runs to the kitchen opening the door and calling in

Eric Norman!

Norman's face appears in the doorway

Norman Norman's dead!

Norman disappears back into the kitchen

Eric (*considering this*) I mean "Willie", Norman's son. Could I have a word?

Norman appears again

Norman I was just about to decant the sherry.

Eric pulls Norman out

Eric (*calling off*) Won't keep him a minute, Mr Jenkins — help yourself to another drinkie-poo.

Eric slams the door

Norman, our situation has deteriorated.
Norman Deteriorated? It's bloody disintegrated.
Eric Shut up. We have *got* to get rid of Mr Jenkins.
Norman How? He's going to stay here until we produce Mrs Swan.
Eric Hell.
Norman And he's almost polished off your cooking sherry.

George sits up, holding his head. He's very confused

George Are my clothes ready yet?
Eric Uncle George!

Eric and Norman rush to George's aid

George (*dazed*) I've got to get all dressed up as you.
Eric Forget that now.
Norman Yes, that's off, you can go home.
George I want to go to bed.

George falls unconscious again into Eric's arms

Norman Come on, Uncle George, don't leave us again.

Norman slaps George in quick succession in an attempt to revive him

Jenkins enters from the kitchen, sherry glass in hand

Jenkins is about to speak, when he sees Norman slapping George. Norman realizes something is wrong and slowly turns to see Jenkins

Jenkins What on earth are you doing to poor Mr Swan?

Norman Putting some colour back into his cheeks.

Jenkins Mr Bassett you really should leave all that to Mr Forbright, your foster father's undertaker.

Norman Yes, you're absolutely right.

Jenkins Now while I was in the kitchen, something struck me.

Norman It probably fell off the fridge.

Jenkins No, no. (*Loudly, to Norman*) That lady just now. That's Mrs Bassett, your widowed mother?

Norman That's right.

Jenkins I still feel she's far too young to be your mother.

Eric You're right. She's his stepmother.

Norman Oh, my God!

Jenkins (*loudly, to Norman*) Stepmother?

Norman Well, before my father lost his job and the family fell on hard times and I was fostered here by the Swans — —

Jenkins Yes.

Norman — my real mother died and so my father — the lumberjack — remarried. She's my stepmother.

Jenkins Ah, I see. Well, that would explain her lack of respect for your father Norman.

Norman Thank God it explains something.

Jenkins And how did your real mother die?

Norman She was struck while Mum and Dad were felling trees down Petticoat Lane.

Jenkins How awful.

Eric Yes, shocking.

Jenkins polishes off his sherry in one gulp

Now, why don't you help yourself to another couple of sherries.

Jenkins No, three's quite enough for me at this time in the morning. I really think I should contact our Ms Cowper.

Jenkins reaches for the phone but Eric's there before him

Eric No! You don't want to do that.

Jenkins You're right, I don't want to do that. But as there is no sign of your landlady, I should report this to head office.

Eric No! Mrs Swan will be here — within a quarter of an hour.

Jenkins Really?

Norman What?

Eric (*thinking*) Yes. I contacted her at work and she's on her way home right now.

Jenkins I'm pleased to hear it.

Eric So you can have a nice pot of tea ready for her by the time she arrives.

Jenkins By the way, Mrs Swan's washing machine is making a very funny noise.

Eric If you can fix it for her, she'll be very grateful.

Jenkins (*enthusiastically*) Oooh, right. I'll have a go at that.

Jenkins hurries into the kitchen

Norman How the hell can we introduce Mr Jenkins to Mrs Swan — you're never going to persuade Linda to help you out! And anyway, he thinks she's my loopy widowed stepmother who eats the wallpaper.

Eric I know, that's why we're going to revive Uncle George, dress him up in stockings, bra, corset, maternity dress and a long blonde wig, then pass him off as Mrs Swan.

Norman thinks he's joking

Norman That's very funny — maternity dress and a long blonde wig. That's very good. (*He laughs, but then he realizes*) Oh, my *God*!

Eric (*still struggling with Uncle George*) Help me with Uncle George.

Norman You can't be serious? Pass off Uncle George as your wife?

Eric Not *my* wife, I'm Mr Thompson, remember? Uncle George will be Mr *Swan's* wife — widow.

Norman Well, who's going to be *Mr* Swan, then?

Eric Nobody, Mr Swan's dead.

Norman I can't keep up with this!

Eric Now — smelling salts?

Norman (*indicates the rubbish bag*) I told you we haven't got any. I thought we could use this to bring him round. It's got yesterday's cat food in it.

They smell the rubbish bag

Eric ⎫ (*together*) Ough!
Norman ⎭

Norman Come on, let's get him in.

Eric and Norman attempt to feed George's head into the plastic bag. In their struggles, they hold George upside-down in the bag

> *Forbright enters from the dining-room, astonished and aghast at what Norman and Eric are attempting to do. They do not notice Forbright, until — —*

Forbright Gentlemen!

Eric and Norman stop dead

> What in God's name are you doing with Mr Bassett?

Eric and Norman still hold George upside-down in the bag

Norman I — er — thought that if we did it ourselves, we could save on the funeral expenses.
Forbright What?
Eric And quicker too, dustbins go out tonight.
Forbright Mr Bassett, being thrown out with the rubbish is hardly a dignified manner for your dear father to depart this world.
Eric (*to Norman*) I told you he wouldn't go for it, Willie.

They lower George as Forbright steps closer and indicates the dining-room

Forbright Now, Mr Bassett, we are ready for your father.
Norman No!
Forbright We'll lay him peacefully on the dining-room table.
Norman You mustn't take him in there.
Forbright And why not?
Norman Because — er —
Eric Because Willie suddenly remembered that his mother's having a dinner party tonight.
Norman That'll do.
Forbright I beg your pardon?
Norman I said, it's going to be quite a do.
Forbright A dinner party?
Eric Yes, Mrs Bassett is having a few close friends for dinner and it wouldn't look right if *Mr* Bassett was the centrepiece, would it?
Forbright Mr Bassett, I think it would be easier for everyone if I simply took your father with me now back to my funeral parlour.

Eric and Norman block off Forbright's advance

Eric ⎫ (*together*) No!
Norman ⎭
Forbright Gentlemen, please — —

Norman takes George in his arms

Norman (*interrupting*) No, no you mustn't take Daddy away. Not until the rest of the family have paid their last respects.
Forbright Rest of your family?

Each time Norman falters, Eric whispers help

Norman Yes. They'll all have to say "goodbye". There's — er — —
Eric Grandmother, Norman.
Norman — dear old Granny Norma, up in the back room. And — er — —
Eric Sister, Rosemary
Norman — sister Rosie, down in the basement. And — er — —
Eric Brother, Bertie.
Norman — and my dear brother, Bertie.
Forbright Bertie Bassett?
Norman (*giving Eric a look*) Yes. And it was my father's dying wish that they should all pay their last respects in this house.
Forbright But where shall we lay him out then?
Eric Let's put him in one of the bedrooms upstairs.
Forbright Very well, I shall move everything up there.
Eric Thank you, most kind.

Eric turns Forbright as, behind them, George is suddenly awake in Norman's arms

George (*foolishly*) Hallo.

George falls unconscious again as Forbright turns to Norman, who waves coyly

Norman (*foolishly*) Hallo.
Forbright (*politely*) Good-morning, Mr Bassett.

Forbright turns away again and George is awake

George (*holding his head*) That bloody door!

Forbright turns back quickly as George faints again. Norman sees the kitchen door

Norman That bloody door! That awful, horrible, bloody door, I hate it! I
want it out of here, it's a terrible thing — you can bury it along with Dad.
Forbright You can't bury a door!
Eric You're right, we'll cremate it instead.

Eric pushes Forbright off into the dining-room

Norman immediately tries to revive George but he's fully unconscious again.
Eric grabs the clothes from the box in the cupboard

Norman Come on, Uncle George. Oh, it's no good. Look at him — he'll
never be able to pretend to be your wife.
Eric You're right, Norman. At least one of us is still thinking straight.
Norman Thank you.
Eric We'll have to abandon the idea of Uncle George impersonating Linda.
Norman Thank heavens for that.
Eric Yes, *you'll* have to do it instead.
Norman I knew you'd see it clearly in the — *(realizing) I'll* have to do it!

Eric pushes the various articles of clothing into Norman's hands. Norman
tries to interject but Eric is in full swing, during — —

Eric Come on, there's no time to lose. Mr Jenkins will never recognize you
under this lot, and he's had a few sherries too. It's windy out there so you
can tie a scarf around your head. Not even Brenda would know who it was.
Norman Oh, God, Brenda.

Linda enters from the bedroom

Norman stuffs the clothes up his front

Linda Eric!
Eric Yes, dear?
Linda Dr Chapman wants to see us in the bedroom *now*!

Dr Chapman appears in the doorway

Dr Chapman What I actually suggested was that I come back next — —
Linda Now!
Eric We still have guests.
Norman You still have guests.
Linda *NOW*!
Dr Chapman Excuse me.

Dr Chapman scuttles back into the bedroom

Linda You've got five minutes, then I'm evicting the lot of them myself.
Eric Well, Norman was just leaving, weren't you, Norman?
Norman (*indicating his stomach*) Yes. I was just going to take an Alka Seltzer.

Eric pushes Norman off as — —

Sally enters from the dining-room with a bundle of table-cloths

Sally Excuse me.
Linda (*to Sally*) You, out!
Sally Look, I don't know who you are, but you're not making what I have to do any easier.
Linda I'm Norman's landlady.
Sally Well, I'm dealing with him as fast as I can.
Linda Oh, that's nice, isn't it?
Eric Very.

Sally starts towards the UR *arch*

Sally If you don't mind.
Linda Where are you going with those?
Sally I'm going upstairs to lay Norman.

Eric nearly dies as Linda looks amazed

Linda You're going to do what?
Sally Lay Norman in the bed.
Linda What?
Sally We were going to do it on the dining-room table.

Eric dies again

But now I've got to hump him upstairs.
Linda And then just leave him.
Sally I suppose so.
Linda You heartless tart.
Sally Heartless tart?
Eric (*to Sally*) Yes, heartless tart — I think it's a pudding she's making.
Sally Oh!

Sally storms out through the UR *arch as — —*

Forbright enters from the dining-room

Forbright Almost ready.
Eric Good.
Forbright I hope young Mr Bassett will be all right — I think the shock has
   affected him more than he'd care to admit.
Eric Yes, I think it has.
Linda What shock?

Eric tries to push Linda back to the bedroom

Eric It doesn't matter.

Linda pulls free of Eric and steps to Forbright

Linda What's happened?
Eric Nothing that concerns you, darling.
Forbright Mr Bassett's father died.
Eric Oh, bloody hell.
Linda Mr Bassett's father?
Eric Died, apparently.
Forbright This morning.
Eric Yes, Mr Bassett popped over after you left and just dropped down dead.
Linda Good heavens — Norman didn't say anything.
Forbright Norman didn't say anything ...

Eric shoots a look at Forbright

Eric Er — no. No, I don't think he did. No, no, Norman didn't say a word,
   he just came up the garden path ...

*Eric mimes knocking on a door, opening a door, waving hallo and dying on
the spot*

Linda Oh, dear. (*To Forbright*) What did Mr Bassett die of?
Eric Lassa Fever.
Forbright (*suddenly very worried*) Lassa Fever?
Linda My God, that explains why the Health Department have been here all
   morning.
Eric Yes, that's right. It was all very sudden.
Forbright Sudden?
Eric It took all of us completely by surprise.
Linda It certainly has.

Forbright But with Lassa Fever, surely poor Mr Bassett would have been bedridden for weeks?

Eric Well, he was.

Forbright But you just said it was sudden.

Eric That's right.

Forbright But he must have been dying for some time now.

Eric Yes, he was. He was dying for ages. But the bit right at the end — the very end — that was bloody sudden. That last moment, lights on, lights off, just like that. Very sudden.

He drops down dead on the spot again

Forbright (*anxious*) I see, but sir, Lassa Fever is highly contagious!

Eric (*worried*) Is it?

Forbright You don't understand, this changes everything.

Eric (*more worried*) Does it?

Forbright Definitely — there's an entirely different code of practice when dealing with a contagious disease.

Eric (*extremely worried*) Is there?

Forbright Mr Bassett's body has to be sealed and sent for autopsy as soon as possible!

Eric (*horrified*) Autopsy?

Forbright Immediately!

Eric takes this in. Finally, he turns to Linda

Eric (*calmly*) How about we go out for lunch?

Linda Out for lunch?

Eric Great idea! You pop down to that cafe on the corner and I'll meet you there for that little chat.

Linda I'm not going anywhere!

Forbright crosses to the dining-room, but Eric is quickly next to him

Forbright I think I'd better collect the rest of my things.

Eric No! Don't you do anything.

Forbright I have to remove the body this instant.

Eric You mustn't.

Linda (*to Eric*) Did anyone find out what Norman wants?

Eric No, they didn't.

Forbright (*looking down at the unconscious George*) Find out what Norman wants?

Linda Of course.

Eric Absolutely.

Forbright I don't wish to be indelicate but I don't think what Norman wanted is of any consequence.

Linda Don't you?

Forbright I mean it's hardly relevant, is it?

Linda (*indicating George*) You're about to take this man off for an autopsy and you don't care what Norman thinks?

Forbright Not really.

Linda You callous swine!

Forbright Callous swine?

Eric No, "Callus Wine", it's a full-bodied Chablis to go with the heartless tart she's making.

Eric pushes Forbright into the dining-room, then crosses right of Linda, who just looks in amazement at the dining-room door

Linda What a horrible man!

Eric Isn't he just. (*Calling upstairs*) Norman!

Linda Now, perhaps we can spend five minutes with Dr Chapman.

Eric Oh, no, I've got far more important things to do.

George sits up behind Linda's back

George It's time I got all dressed up!

As George falls unconscious again, Linda turns in amazement to Eric

Linda What did you just say?

Eric I said — "It's time I got all dressed up".

Linda bursts into tears and runs into the bedroom

(*To George*) Come on, Uncle George, we've got to keep you out of trouble. Upstairs, no. Kitchen, no! Dining-room, no! Bedroom — oh, hell! (*Then he sees the window-seat*) Ah ha! Come on, Uncle George, it's into the window-seat.

Eric staggers backwards to the window-seat with George as — —

Forbright appears from the dining-room

Forbright then looks on in amazement as Eric attempts to shove George into the window-seat — it's a very tight squeeze. He pushes George's head down but it keeps popping back up. So he gives George's head an almighty slap

Forbright Mr Thompson!
Eric Agh!

Eric slams the window-seat lid and jumps on top of the window-seat, pretending to clean the windows with the curtains

Forbright What on earth are you doing with poor Mr Bassett?
Eric Just seeing if he fits.

Eric measures the window-seat by walking along its lid

Forbright Fits?
Eric Yes, we're going to have a made-to-measure coffin made to measure and I wanted to see what size we needed.
Forbright Mr Thompson!

Eric hands Forbright a cricket bat and several pieces of cricket equipment from the window-seat

Eric And I think we'll need the larger size after all.
Forbright Larger size?
Eric Yes, the biggest coffin you offer, because Mr Bassett requested to be cremated with his cricket gear.
Forbright But what about the ashes?
Eric We'll lose them I expect.

Jenkins enters from the kitchen, sherry bottle in one hand, wooden mallet in the other, his arms covered in foam

Jenkins Mr Thompson, your washing machine is making a very funny noise indeed.
Eric It doesn't matter.
Jenkins But it's starting to foam.

Eric crosses to the kitchen

Eric Oh, bloody hell.
Forbright (*indicating window-seat*) Mr Thompson, you should take poor Mr Bassett out.
Eric No, leave him there, he might as well start getting used to it.

Eric and Jenkins exit to the kitchen as — —

Sally enters from the UR *arch*

Sally Nearly ready for him.
Forbright Change of plan, Miss Chessington.
Sally Oh, not again.
Forbright Most urgent, I have to make plans to have the body sealed prior to autopsy.
Sally Autopsy?
Forbright And they need a larger coffin for his equipment.

Forbright hands her the cricket stump, which Sally looks at with a wry smile

Forbright then opens the door to reveal Ms Cowper standing there — a severe looking DSS inspector. Ms Cowper is wearing a raincoat, a scarf around her head and carrying a briefcase

Good-morning.
Ms Cowper I doubt that.

She steps in uninvited and Forbright closes the door

Are you Mr Thompson?
Forbright Er — no.
Ms Cowper Swan?
Forbright No.
Ms Cowper Bassett?
Forbright No. Forbright.
Ms Cowper Well, Mr Forbright, my name is Ms Cowper.
Forbright Miss Cowper.
Ms Cowper *Ms, Ms* Cowper. Department of Social Security, Chief Borough Inspector. I believe our man Jenkins has been here all morning.
Forbright Jenkins?
Ms Cowper Checking up on your Mr Thompson.
Forbright Ah, well, Mr Thompson is in the kitchen at the moment with a gentleman from the Health Department.

Eric backs out of the kitchen, bubbles floating everywhere

Eric (*calling, off*) Stop complaining and just keep your thumb in that hole!
Forbright Ah, Mr Thompson, this lady has arrived to see you.
Eric (*not interested*) All right. No, your thumb!
Forbright And in the meantime, I'll take Miss Chessington and see if I can get my hands on a larger one.

Forbright and Sally leave

Eric shuts the kitchen door and turns to Ms Cowper. He looks her up and down. Bursts into laughter — finally he slaps her on the back

Eric (*to Ms Cowper*) You look marvellous!
Ms Cowper I beg your pardon?
Eric That's brilliant! (*imitating her*) "I beg your pardon?" (*Then normally again*) Fabulous. I'd never have known.
Ms Cowper What?
Eric (*imitating her again*) "What?" Ha! We've got nothing to worry about.
Ms Cowper Nothing to worry about?
Eric (*imitating her again*) "Nothing to worry about"! (*He points to her chest*) You don't think those are a bit — er — you know ... (*he indicates that her chest might be a bit large*)
Ms Cowper Oh!
Eric Oh, one thing — don't get too close, your moustache is beginning to show.
Ms Cowper Mr Thompson!
Eric (*imitating her*) "Mr Thompson"! But these are great. (*He prods her chest*) Hey, look at that — they wobble and everything.

Eric wobbles her chest and moves Ms Cowper so that his back is to the stairs. Eric puts his face right in Ms Cowper's chest and shakes his cheeks about

Norman hurries in from the UR *arch holding the dress*

Eric turns to Norman with a beaming smile — gives him a nod of "Well done" and puts his face back in Ms Cowper's chest. Then Eric stops dead. Horrified

Norman goes to speak, thinks better of it, then dashes back off the way he came

Eric is motionless. He looks at Ms Cowper, who glares back at him

Jenkins enters from the kitchen, thick foam all over his shirt and trousers, carrying the sherry bottle

Jenkins Ms Cowper!

Eric stops dead. He looks blank for a moment as his mind whirls, then he emits a nervous giggle as he turns to the stone-faced Ms Cowper, trying desperately to lighten the moment

Ms Cowper Mr Thompson, what was the meaning of what occurred just now?

Eric I was just trying to keep abreast of events.

Ms Cowper I saw!

Eric Ms Cowper, you'll have to forgive me. I've been under a lot of strain this morning.

Ms Cowper That is no excuse. You were a witness to this, Jenkins.

Eric No, you don't understand, I suffer from Tourette's Syndrome.

Ms Cowper Tourette's Syndrome?

Jenkins The uncontrollable urge to shout out insults at people.

Eric That's right, thank you, Mr Jenkins. (*Then to Ms Cowper*) Well, in the final stages of Tourette's Syndrome, the sufferer never knows if he's going to simply insult people or actually physically abuse complete strangers.

Ms Cowper Heavens.

Eric It can be very embarrassing.

Jenkins No, I've read several medical papers on the subject and I don't recall anything about physical abuse.

Eric It's absolutely true, Big Boy!

Eric suddenly gooses Jenkins

Jenkins Aaaagh!

Eric Whoa! There I go again!

Ms Cowper Really, Mr Thompson!

Eric (*to Ms Cowper*) Oh, shut up and give us a feel!

Eric goes for Ms Cowper's chest again, and she slaps his hands away

Ms Cowper Get off me!

Eric I'm sorry! I can't apologize enough. It's got much worse of late.

Ms Cowper and Jenkins move closer to him

I mean it just used to be ... (*He waves his hand limply in the air*) But now it's — Hagh! (*He gooses both of them*)

They scream

I'm sorry, I'm sorry — I'll try and keep my mouth shut and my hands to myself.

Ms Cowper If you could. (*Then she crosses to Jenkins, giving Eric a wide berth*) Now Jenkins, were you able to get Mr Swan's confirmation on Mr Thompson's illness?

Jenkins No. Mr Swan wasn't here.

Ms Cowper Well, where is he?

Jenkins He's dead.

Ms Cowper Dead?

Eric That's right.

Ms Cowper Mr Swan is dead?

Eric Yes, poor old Mr Swan passed away this morning, which is why he couldn't sign my forms.

Ms Cowper Really.

Eric But there is no need to worry as *Mrs* Swan is on her way back here to sign them instead. So you can return to Head Office, knowing that Jenkins here is very much in charge of the situation.

Ms Cowper steps out of Eric's grip

Ms Cowper Mr Thompson, I do not like being played with.

Eric (*offhand*) So I noticed.

Ms Cowper You're not dealing with Jenkins now, you know.

Eric No indeed.

Ms Cowper I'm not easy to satisfy.

Eric (*offhand*) I can imagine that.

Ms Cowper When Mrs Swan gets here, she will find herself answerable to some very direct questions concerning her numerous lodgers.

Eric She'll be more than happy to help you.

Ms Cowper And where are all the lodgers — this appears a dreadfully quiet home for such a houseful.

Eric Everyone tends to keep themselves to themselves.

Jenkins And there have been *two* deaths here this morning.

Ms Cowper *Two* deaths?

Eric Thank you, Mr Jenkins.

Jenkins Yes, Mr *Bassett* passed away this morning, as well as Mr Swan.

Eric Quite right, Mr Jenkins. Thank you, Mr Jenkins.

Jenkins Norman Bassett fell out of a tree.

Ms Cowper Mr Bassett, the lumberjack, fell out of a tree?

Eric Yes. Norman was up in the tree, having a bit of practice before the winter set in, when a branch snapped and he fell to his death.

Ms Cowper is having a very hard time believing any of this

Ms Cowper And has anybody else died?

Eric No. Absolutely not.

Jenkins Not unless you count Willie-Dickie's first mother.

Eric Oh, God!

Ms Cowper Willie-Dickie's first mother?
Jenkins Yes, she was killed while felling trees down Petticoat Lane.

Ms Cowper gives him a stern look

Apparently.
Ms Cowper So where is Mrs Bassett, Norman's widow?
Jenkins Ah, yes, I believe she's been locked securely away.

Ms Cowper turns slowly to give Jenkins another stern look

It's that time again.
Ms Cowper That time?
Jenkins Yes — her moon's in Uranus.

Ms Cowper just looks at Jenkins

Eric Mrs Bassett's become very upset since she heard that her husband fell out of a tree.
Jenkins Mrs Bassett eats the wallpaper if they don't lock her up.

Linda enters from the bedroom, completely furious!

Linda Get in here now!
Jenkins (*urgently, to Ms Cowper*) My God, she's got out again.

Dr Chapman hurries in from the bedroom

Dr Chapman I really don't think this is the best atmosphere for an intimate family discussion.
Linda Sit down.
Dr Chapman (*sitting*) Certainly.
Linda (*indicating Ms Cowper*) Who's this?!
Eric She's with Mr Jenkins, the gentleman from the dining-room.

Linda crosses to Jenkins and Ms Cowper

Linda Haven't you done enough spraying for one day?
Ms Cowper I beg your pardon?
Jenkins Watch her, Ms Cowper — remember Uranus.
Ms Cowper Jenkins!
Eric Yes. Thank you, Mr Jenkins. You must remember she's having a terrible day, Ms Cowper.

Jenkins (*sympathetically*) Yes, her poor husband.
Ms Cowper (*also sympathetic*) Yes, of course.
Linda (*to Jenkins*) What about my husband?
Eric (*to Linda*) Nothing. It's just very sad, that's all.
Jenkins You have our condolences.
Linda But how on earth did you find out about it?
Jenkins Mr Swan telephoned our department this morning.
Linda He did what?
Eric Telephoned the department. Just wanted to let them know.
Linda Let them know?
Jenkins That your poor husband had gone like that.
Linda (*to Eric*) Talk about getting it out in the open!
Dr Chapman Yes, in some cases a public declaration can be very beneficial.

They all look at him

I'll sit down, shall I? (*He sits*)
Jenkins It's an odd way to go, but perfectly natural.
Linda A natural way to go?
Jenkins I believe my grandfather went the same way during the First World War.
Linda Well, I don't want my husband to go "that" way!
Eric Don't upset yourself.
Linda How can you say that? You're a cross-dresser!
Eric Cross? I'm bloody furious!

Linda bursts into tears and runs to the bedroom as — —

Dr Chapman (*wagging an accusing finger at Eric*) You have a lot of explaining to do, Uncle George.
Jenkins Uncle George?
Eric (*picking up from Jenkins*) Uncle George?

The doorbell rings

Dr Chapman Excuse me.

Dr Chapman hurries into the bedroom

The doorbell rings again

Ms Cowper (*indicating that Jenkins should go and open the door*) Jenkins.
Jenkins Of course.

There's a rapid knocking as Jenkins goes for the front door

Eric No! Allow me!

But it's too late, Jenkins opens the door to reveal Brenda, Norman's girl-next-door fiancée. She's quite distraught

Jenkins Good-morning.
Brenda I'm looking for Norman.
Jenkins Norman?
Ms Cowper Norman Bassett?
Brenda Yes, I'm Brenda Dixon.
Eric Brenda!
Brenda Yes, I'm Brenda, Norman's fiancée.
Eric Oh, bloody hell.
Ms Cowper Norman's what?
Brenda (*to Ms Cowper*) Are you Mrs Swan?
Ms Cowper No, I am not, young lady.
Brenda (*to Jenkins*) Mr Swan?
Jenkins No, madam.

Brenda crosses quickly to Eric

Brenda Mr Swan?
Eric No, I'm Rupert Thompson. And this is Mr Jenkins. I believe you've met Ms Cowper, Mr Jenkins, Ms Cowper — —
Ms Cowper Mr Thompson!
Eric — correct, Mr Thompson. Thank you, Ms Cowper, Mr Jenkins. Mr Jenkins, Ms Cowper. Ms Cowper, Miss Dixon. Miss Dixon — —
Brenda I've been phoning all morning. Norman didn't show up for work apparently.
Jenkins (*sympathetically*) I think you'd better sit down, miss.

Eric tries to lead Brenda away

Eric No. Why don't you go home, Brenda, and we'll fill you in later.
Brenda (*pulling away from Eric*) No, I'm very worried about Norman. He was talking gibberish on the phone. I must see him.
Jenkins That must have been just before it occurred.
Eric Yes.
Brenda I must see him.
Jenkins I really think she should sit down.
Eric No, she shouldn't, you ugly old trout!

Eric gooses Jenkins. Ms Cowper steps in to Brenda

Ms Cowper You say you're Norman Bassett's fiancée?
Brenda That's right. We're getting married on Saturday. Where is he?
Ms Cowper Married on Saturday?
Brenda St Mary's at twelve o'clock and I've got the most beautiful dress.
Ms Cowper Mr Norman Bassett at this address.
Brenda Yes.
Ms Cowper But Mr Bassett is already married.
Eric Oh, God!

Brenda takes this in

Brenda Already married?
Ms Cowper Correct.
Brenda (*showing off her engagement ring*) No. There must be some sort of a mistake.
Eric (*trying to lead Brenda away again*) Yes. Some sort of a mistake — that would explain it.
Jenkins No, it's all in the file, Mr Bassett's been married for several years now.

Brenda starts to take this in

Eric Anybody like a nice cup of tea?
Brenda Oh — my — God!
Jenkins You didn't know?
Brenda Of course I didn't know. I'd never have got engaged to him if I'd known he had a wife!
Ms Cowper This is his second wife, actually.
Brenda Second wife?
Jenkins His first wife was killed in a tree-felling accident.
Brenda What?
Jenkins In Petticoat Lane.
Brenda I can't believe I'm hearing any of this.
Eric I know how you feel — I mean who would have expected this from Norman.
Brenda (*wailing*) Norman!
Jenkins Mr Thompson, someone should inform Norman's son that this lady's arrived.
Eric I'm not sure that's a good idea.
Brenda (*utterly gob-smacked now*) Son?
Eric No, definitely not a good idea, Mr Jenkins.

Brenda (*to Jenkins*) Norman's son?
Jenkins Miss Dixon.
Brenda Yes.
Jenkins Norman's got a little Willie.

Brenda screams!

Ms Cowper Jenkins, sit her down.

Jenkins sits Brenda on the sofa

Brenda Thank you.
Eric No, she *can't* sit down.
Jenkins The poor girl's in shock, for heaven's sake.
Eric We all are. (*He tries to lead her away*) But she should go home now and discuss it in the morning with Mrs Bassett.
Brenda (*wailing*) Mrs Bassett!
Eric Oh, shut up — it's not all that bad.
Jenkins Not all that bad? She just discovered her fiancé was attempting bigamy!
Brenda (*wailing and collapsing in Jenkins' arms*) Bigamy!
Ms Cowper It seemed to be finding out about her fiancé's little Willie that set her off.
Brenda I want to see Norman now.
Eric No, that's impossible.
Brenda Why? Where is he?
Eric He's — er — he's gone.
Brenda Gone?
Jenkins (*to Eric*) Will you tell her, or should I?
Eric No-one should tell her, you big fart!

He gooses Jenkins

Ms Cowper Mr Thompson!
Eric Cor! Lovely, lovely, lovely!!

Eric grabs Ms Cowper's chest

   Sorry, sorry, sorry!
Brenda (*worried*) Tell me what?
Eric (*trying to be nonchalant*) Nothing, nothing at all. Norman's just gone, that's all

Jenkins puts his arm around Brenda's shoulders in a fatherly fashion

Jenkins Brenda?
Brenda Yes?
Jenkins Norman is dead.
Eric Oh, my God.
Brenda I beg your pardon?
Jenkins It happened earlier this morning.
Brenda What happened?
Jenkins Norman fell out of a tree.
Brenda (*looking up*) Norman fell out of a tree?
Jenkins Yes.
Brenda (*looking down, very sad*) And died?
Ms Cowper Yes.
Brenda Oh, my God!

She collapses in Jenkins' arms

Eric (*to Ms Cowper*) Now look what you've done, you old bag! And you big prat! Sorry, sorry, sorry!
Brenda (*wailing*) My lovely Norman!
Ms Cowper Take her into a bedroom!
Eric (*protecting the way to the bedroom*) No! I'll take her in the dining-room! Give her a stiff drink.
Jenkins Is that a good idea?
Eric Yes, we'll all have one!
Brenda My beautiful Norman!
Eric (*leading Brenda away*) C'mon, there's a drinks cabinet through here.
Brenda Wait a minute. What was Norman doing up in a tree?
Jenkins Well, he was practising before the winter set in.
Brenda Practising what?
Jenkins His job.
Brenda You're telling me that my Norman was up in a tree practising selling shoes?
Jenkins Selling shoes?
Eric Yes, it was a shoe tree.

Eric pulls Brenda off into the dining-room just as — —

Sally and Forbright enter in through the front door, wheeling in a stretcher on a trolley. All four meet in the centre

Ms Cowper (*indicating the stretcher*) What's the meaning of this, Mr Forbright?
Forbright We're removing the body for immediate examination.

Ms Cowper Which one?

Sally Dear departed Norman Bassett.

Forbright Yes. I believe they've been keeping him in the window-seat.

Ms Cowper The window-seat?

Forbright (*opening the window-seat*) Ah, yes, it's still here. (*Then, indicating Jenkins*) I'm sure the gentleman from the Health Department wouldn't approve.

Ms Cowper Gentleman from the Health Department?

Ms Cowper looks at Jenkins, who looks around for the "gentleman from the Health Department" and is utterly lost. As Ms Cowper pulls Jenkins down stage, Sally and Forbright take the still unconscious George, and place him on the stretcher. Then they cover George with a long sheet and strap him down at his head, feet and securely around the middle, arms in, during the following ——

Ms Cowper Jenkins, come here! What in God's name has been happening here this morning?

Jenkins What, all of it?

Ms Cowper Certainly all of it.

Jenkins Well. (*He takes a swig from the sherry bottle*) Agh! (*Then, unstopping and with gusto!*) After I arrived and the gout-ridden Mr Thompson signed for his industrial injuries disablement benefit, Mr Swan wasn't available for confirmation so I was introduced to his foster son, Willie-Dickie John Thomas, a deaf, unemployed piano-tuner. Then, having pursued Mr Swan to the roof and back, we discovered that he had in fact died earlier this morning having been struck by a solid oak door, so Mrs Swan was sent for. That just about brings you up to date apart from Willie-Dickie's recently bereaved stepmother who eats the wallpaper when her moon's in Uranus and her late, bigamist husband who fell out of a shoe tree while attempting to do a little pruning before the winter set in.

Ms Cowper That's easy for you to say.

Sally and Forbright stand up, supporting the stretchered George between them

Forbright Right, we'll be off then.

Eric enters from the dining-room with a tray of sherries as ——

Sally and Forbright start towards the door with George on the trolley

Eric All right, who's for a little snifter? (*He sees Sally, Forbright and George*) No!

Eric throws the sherries back into the dining-room. CRASH! Then he races to stop the stretcher

What do you think you're doing?

Forbright I told you, Mr Thompson, with a contagious disease, Mr Bassett's body has to be removed for immediate autopsy.

Eric You can't autopsy poor old Norman!

Forbright and Sally start to exit again; Eric struggles with them

Ms Cowper Contagious disease? You just said that Mr Bassett fell out of a tree.

Sally No, it was Lassa Fever. (*Then, to Eric*) Let go of him, Mr Thompson!

Eric He doesn't want to leave yet!

Forbright We have to get him to the hospital.

Eric Tell you what, to save time, you two go ahead, and I'll just chuck Norman on the bonfire.

Forbright ⎫ (*together*) Bonfire!
Sally   ⎭

Jenkins Mr Thompson, you should leave everything to Mr Forbright, here.

Eric leaps over George to deal with Jenkins and Ms Cowper, ushering them towards the kitchen. Forbright and Sally head to the front door with George

Eric Mr Jenkins, why don't you just show Ms Cowper your washing machine and I'll be with you in three minutes.

Ms Cowper I have no wish to see the washing machine!

Eric Then give us a quick feel, wobble, wobble, wobble!

Eric grabs Ms Cowper's chest

Ms Cowper Aagh!

Ms Cowper hurries off into the kitchen

Jenkins Really, Mr Thompson!

Eric God, you've got a lovely bottom!

Eric gooses Jenkins and he yells and runs off into the kitchen

For a moment, Sally pulls the stretcher through the front door — out of view of the audience. Forbright remains in the doorway — in this instant the

"George stretcher" is substituted with a "dummy stretcher" which looks identical to the original

Eric runs to Sally and Forbright

  Stop! No, you mustn't!

There's a crash as if the trolley has fallen over

Forbright Now look what you've done!

Eric pulls the dummy stretcher back through the front door, struggling with Forbright and Sally

Sally He's off his trolley!
Eric Bloody do-gooder!
Forbright You're being very silly, Mr Thompson!
Eric Leave him in peace.
Sally Much more of this and he'll leave in pieces!

Eric manages to drag them back into the room

Eric I told you, he doesn't want to go!
Forbright And I told you, we have to dispose of the body!

In their struggle, they drop the dummy stretcher on its back with a crash

Eric Now look what you've done!
Forbright Gracious!

Eric picks up the dummy stretcher at its head and stands it upright

Eric Well, excuse me, but if this is the sort of treatment poor Mr Bassett can expect, I would sooner choose another undertaker — —
Forbright (*furious*) Mr Thompson!
Eric What?

Eric steps aside and the dummy stretcher falls forward onto its front, so it is now face down

Forbright No!
Eric Right, that's it. You're fired.
Forbright You can't fire the undertaker!

Sally and Forbright start to pick up the stretcher once more

Brenda (screaming) stumbles out of the dining-room with a decanter of brandy, causing them to drop the stretcher once again

Sally No!
Brenda My lovely Norman! He was so young!
Eric There's plenty more fish in the sea.
Forbright (*referring to the dummy stretcher*) Up we go again.

Brenda sees Sally and Forbright with the dummy stretcher

Brenda Who's that?
Eric That's nobody.
Forbright This is the late Norman Bassett.
Eric Oh, bloody hell.
Brenda (*running to the stretcher*) Oh, Norman! No! Don't leave me!
Forbright Behave yourself!
Eric Yes, pull yourself together, Brenda!

In her anguish and pain, Brenda thumps her fists into the dummy

Brenda My lovely, lovely Norman.
Eric Get him out of here!
Sally But I thought you said ——
Eric Just do as you're told!
Brenda Norman, one last kiss!

Brenda starts to pull the sheet off, but Eric pulls her away

Eric No! She mustn't see what's under the sheet.
Brenda Why not?
Eric Because Norman's all ...

Eric pulls an ugly mutated face

Brenda screams and runs back into the dining-room

Sally and Forbright start towards the front door again with the dummy stretcher

Sally Right then.
Eric No!

Forbright What now?

Ms Cowper enters from the kitchen

Ms Cowper (*sternly*) Mr Thompson!
Eric (*to Forbright*) Drive safely.
Forbright The autopsy will be at St Pancras' Hospital.
Eric In a couple of hours though.
Forbright (*as he goes*) Yes, followed immediately by the cremation.

Forbright exits

Eric Good. (*Then, realizing*) Cremation!

Ms Cowper joins Eric at the front door

Ms Cowper Mr Thompson!
Eric Ms Cowper.
Ms Cowper It was not my morning's intention to watch our Mr Jenkins fiddling with your washing machine.
Eric Of course not, Ms Cowper.
Ms Cowper So when will Mrs Swan, your landlady, be here?
Norman (*off, in a fair female voice*) Halloee!

Norman enters from the UR *stairs arch as "Mrs Swan". Norman's wearing a large, floral maternity dress, dark stockings and the blonde wig*

Eric Ah, come on in, Mrs Swan!

Norman, Eric and Ms Cowper meet in the centre

Norman (*in his normal voice*) I was told —— —

Eric gooses him

(*In a high voice*) I was told there was a Mr Jenkins looking for me.
Eric First things first.

Then, introducing Norman to Ms Cowper

This lady is my landlady, Mrs Swan.
Ms Cowper At last.
Eric (*to Norman*) And this lady is Ms Cowper.

Norman (*immediately turning away*) I think I've left something upstairs.
Eric (*stopping him*) No, you haven't.

*Jenkins enters from the kitchen, being chased by a rampant washing
machine churning and crashing after him, Jenkins defends himself with a
plumber's rubber plunger*

Jenkins Get back in there, you beastly thing! Get back!

Jenkins kicks the washing machine back into the kitchen

I hope that washing machine's still under guarantee.

*Jenkins turns back to close the kitchen door and a foam-covered shirt flies
out and hits him in the face*

Eric Thank you, Mr Jenkins, I'm sure you did your best. However, the good
news is Mrs Swan has arrived to sign your papers.
Jenkins Oh, thank the Lord for that. Well, I just have a form for you to sign
— er, I had it a minute ago, then I took it — —

*Jenkins turns to the dining-room, then stops, remembers and looks to the
ceiling*

— Ah.
Ms Cowper Come on, where is it, Jenkins?
Jenkins On the roof.
Ms Cowper The roof?
Jenkins Yes, I left my briefcase up there, when we went to look for the late
Mr Swan.

Norman turns to leave

Norman Oh, well, that's it then, isn't it?
Ms Cowper No, Mrs Swan, I want this matter settled. Jenkins get back up
there and retrieve your briefcase.
Jenkins But it's raining, Ms Cowper.
Ms Cowper Just get up those stairs, Jenkins!

*Ms Cowper snatches the rubber plunger from Jenkins and pushes him up
through the UR arch with the plunger*

Norman pulls off his scarf and wig in fury

Norman I am never helping you out again! That woman could have us both thrown in jail just like that!
Eric Put your wig back on!
Norman No!
Eric She might come back in!
Norman I'm getting out!
Eric In!
Norman Out!

Norman and Eric start to struggle with the wig — and — —

Linda and Dr Chapman enter from the bedroom

Eric and Norman both see Linda together and quickly turn their struggling into a flamboyant dance — the hokey-cokey (in-out, in-out, and shake it all about). Finally, Eric steps away from Norman and smiles, trying to lighten everything

Eric Good-morning again, Doctor. (*To Linda*) Hallo, darling.
Linda Norman.
Norman Yes, Linda?
Linda Why are you wearing a woman's dress and dancing with my husband?
Eric No trick questions please.

Linda shoots Eric a look

Norman Ah, no, it's not a dress, these are my workout clothes.
Linda What?
Norman We were just getting a little exercise. Twenty minutes of aerobics every morning.

Norman performs a couple of jumping jacks. Norman looks sternly at Eric and he joins in

Linda (*not believing a word*) Norman!

They stop the exercises

Norman, that is a very pretty, floral dress.
Norman What, this old thing?
Dr Chapman Now, if Eric's Uncle Norman is a transvestite as well ...
Eric
Linda } (*together*) Sit down!
Norman

Dr Chapman (*sitting*) Certainly.

Linda advances on Eric and Norman

Linda I know what you've been doing with the wigs and the dresses and the stockings.

Eric ⎫
Norman ⎭ (*together*) What?

Linda Yes!
Eric God!
Norman No!
Linda I've found out what you've been doing behind my back.

Eric ⎫
Norman ⎭ (*together*) Oh, Linda!

Linda Waiting until I've left for work — and then getting all dressed up in women's clothes and parading up and down in front of the mirror.

Eric and Norman look and freeze in utter dumbstruck confusion. Eric's mind races

Eric (*finally*) Yes. That's exactly what's been going on behind your back.
Norman What?
Linda I knew it!
Eric Yes. I've been trying on women's clothes.
Linda And Uncle George.
Eric Yes. And Uncle George.
Linda And now Norman as well.

Eric quickly puts the wig back on Norman

Eric Yes. And now Norman as — —
Norman (*interrupting*) Ooh, no. Not me, I've got nothing to do with it.
Linda You're going to stand there dressed like that and deny it?
Norman (*determined to set the record straight*) Linda, prepare yourself for a shock.
Eric Norman don't!
Norman Mrs Swan, for the past two years your Eric has been defrauding the DSS and this morning he forced me to dress up like this to impersonate you in order to sign for one of his numerous falsified claims.

Linda considers this and turns accusingly to Eric — then back to Norman

Linda I think I preferred the one about the aerobics class.

Norman What?

Linda Just own up to it, Norman.

Eric Yes, confess to your little oddity.

Norman I haven't got a little oddity!

Dr Chapman Excuse me, this is Norman, the uncle?

Eric
Linda   } (*together*) No!
Norman

Forbright (*off*) Oh, my God!

Sally (*off*) Watch out!

Eric, Norman and Linda turn as there is a crash of dustbins from off UR

Linda What the hell's going on out there?

Another crash

Eric Nothing. Nothing at all.

> *The front door bursts open and George, still tied to the stretcher and covered in a sheet, races in, his legs waddling*
>
> *Moments later Sally and Forbright dash in through the front door*

Forbright Stop that corpse!

Sally You're not well, Mr Bassett!

> *They chase tied-up George around the sofa and back out through the front door. George races off, quickly followed by Forbright and Sally*

Forbright Slow down!

Sally Mind the road, Mr Bassett! It's slippery out there!

We hear car hooters and screeching brakes from UR, *and we hear a car crash into a set of dustbins. We hear a dog barking and a final crash. Eric turns back to Linda*

Eric Now, what was that you were saying?

> *Ms Cowper bursts back in through the* UR *arch*

Norman shoves his wig back on back to front

Ms Cowper (*shouting off behind her*) Just hold on, you stupid little man!
Eric What's happened?

Ms Cowper moves down to beside Dr Chapman

Ms Cowper The wind blew the attic door shut and Jenkins is stuck out on
  the roof.
Dr Chapman (*to Ms Cowper, standing right in front of her*) Ah, now you
  must be Eric's transsexual Uncle Norman.
Ms Cowper (*glaring*) Sit down.

Dr Chapman sits and Ms Cowper crosses to the UR *stairs*

  (*Shouting out the front door*) Just keep a firm grip of that lightning
  conductor!

Ms Cowper moves to the others. Norman faces the UL *corner*

  (*To Norman*) I think he's broken some tiles, Mrs Swan.
Linda It doesn't matter.
Eric Yeah, never mind the tiles.
Ms Cowper (*to Norman, insistent*) Mrs Swan?
Linda Yes!
Ms Cowper I'm not talking to you, madam.
Linda Yes, you were.
Ms Cowper (*indicating Norman*) I'm talking to Mrs Swan, here.

Linda turns to Norman, becoming more and more upset

Linda Mrs Swan?
Norman I beg your pardon.
Linda Mrs Swan!
Eric Now calm down.
Linda Mrs bloody Swan! You couple of perverts!
Ms Cowper Gracious!
Linda (*to Norman*) You need professional help, Norman!
Norman The sooner the better.
Ms Cowper Norman?
Linda That's right.

Linda pulls off Norman's wig, almost in tears again

  This is Norman Bassett our upstairs lodger.

Eric Oh, my God!

Ms Cowper (*indicating Norman*) This man has been dressing up and impersonating Mrs Swan for the past two years.

Linda Two years! How could you, Eric?

Eric Things are not what they seem, love.

Ms Cowper Eric?

Linda Yes, this is Eric Swan, my husband.

Norman Oh, my God.

Ms Cowper I thought Eric Swan was dead.

Eric Stick around.

Linda What's going on, Eric?

Ms Cowper It's very clear, Mrs Swan, the police will have to be notified.

Eric ⎫
          ⎬ (*together*) The police?
Norman ⎭

Linda The police?

Eric and Norman cuddle in fear

Ms Cowper Yes, your husband's been caught in the act of fiddling with your lodger.

Linda takes this in and turns to see Eric and Norman together

Linda Oh — my — God!

Linda runs to the front door and opens it, just as George runs in — still strapped to the stretcher

Linda and George run into each other and scream! Linda runs to the sofa. George runs across to the dining-room, just as — —

Brenda enters through the dining-room door. Brenda comes face to face with the walking stretcher and screams! George turns and comes face to face with Dr Chapman

Dr Chapman screams and exits through the front door

George runs blind into the kitchen, — screams (off) and crashes (off) into a dresser of plates

Eric (*explaining Uncle George to Ms Cowper*) I think he's come to fix the washing machine.

Norman tries to sneak away but Brenda sees him

Brenda Norman!

Caught in a dress, Norman turns back to her

Norman Hallo, Brenda.

Brenda runs to Norman

Brenda (*delighted*) Norman, you're not dead.
Norman The day's not over yet — Now, you're probably wondering why
   I'm dressed like this — —
Brenda No, I'm game if you are.

She gives Norman a huge happy kiss

Linda I thought that awful woman was Brenda.
Eric I'm not sure where she fits in, actually.

Ms Cowper crosses ominously to Eric and Norman

Ms Cowper Mr Swan and Mr Bassett. There's enough evidence in Mr
   Jenkins' briefcase to put you two in prison for at least ten years!
Norman Oh, no!
Eric It's all right, Norman.
Brenda Prison?
Linda What's Mr Jenkins' briefcase got to do with it, Eric?
Brenda Eric? He said his name was Rupert Thompson.
Norman He's said rather a lot of things today.
Linda Rupert Thompson?
Eric I never meant it to happen like this, Linda.
Linda Never meant what to happen, Eric?

*Eric opens his mouth to speak, when the lights dim and there is a flash of
lightning and an almighty clap of thunder*

Jenkins (*off*) Haa-ahg!
Ms Cowper My God! Jenkins is out on the roof — and so is the briefcase!

*Thunder booms — Norman opens the window and Eric, Norman and Ms
Cowper look out and up at the roof*

As Jenkins' scream stops, Eric and Norman look back in pain

Stay where you are, Jenkins!
Linda What's going on, Eric?
Ms Cowper You hold tight to that briefcase!
Eric You hold tight to that lightning conductor!
Norman And don't worry! Lightning never strikes the same place twice!

There is another flash of lightning and boom of thunder, Jenkins howls and they watch aghast as the entire fileful of papers showers down outside the window — hundreds and hundreds of multi-coloured papers scattered by the wind. The papers are blown all over the stage through the window. Norman and Brenda start ripping up paper

Ms Cowper My evidence!
Norman (*turning back inside*) Oh dear, oh dear.
Ms Cowper Get out of that tree, Jenkins!
Norman It looks like your assets are blowing in the wind, Ms Cowper.
Ms Cowper Get my papers, Jenkins!
Norman What a pity, Ms Cowper, all your evidence has gone.
Linda What evidence?
Norman (*about to tell another whopper*) Well, Linda, it's like this. When the Health Department discovered that the Lassa Fever was spreading into —
Eric (*turning back inside, indicating the strewn papers*) No, Norman, don't, look at this mess. I can't keep this up any longer. Miss Cowper — —
Norman Eric, don't! She's got nothing against you now.
Eric I have to.
Norman You'll go to jail.
Eric I can't live with all these lies. It'll be for the best, Norman — Ms Cowper — I confess.
Ms Cowper You confess?
Linda Confess to what?
Eric I just want you to know, Linda, I never wanted any of this to hurt you.
Linda What's happened?
Eric And Ms Cowper, I have to make one thing perfectly clear, I'm in this on my own, nobody helped me. I blackmailed my Uncle George and my lodger Norman here, into helping me this morning when Mr Jenkins turned up. They're both completely innocent. And as you can see, Norman's not dead. And he's not a lumberjack either.

Brenda and Norman look at his dress

Nor is he married, nor has he ever been married. He hasn't got a father in jail, or any deaf, unemployed children here or anywhere else in the world and he definitely hasn't got a little Willie.

A moment between Brenda and Norman

There's no Mr Thompson living here, with or without gout, nobody with Lassa Fever or any other fever for that matter. There's no pensioners, or children, or widows, or widowers, or single parents, or foster-parents, or divorced parents, or any other sort of parents. (*To Linda, finding the courage*) Linda, I lost my job two years ago — ever since then, I've been defrauding the Department of Social Security. (*To Ms Cowper*) Every one of those claims you received was made up by me. I've done every trick in the book and even written some new ones. And I did it all because I couldn't find work — and I've been able to fool your system for the better part of two years. (*To Linda*) And for everything I've been through, Linda, the worst part of it was having to lie to you.

Linda Oh, Eric.
Eric I just hope that you can find something inside you that can forgive me.
Linda Eric, as long as you love me, I don't care what you are. Employed or unemployed, I'll always be here for you. For better or for worse, remember?

Eric and Linda kiss and hug, as do Norman and Brenda. Then they all turn to face Ms Cowper

Eric There we are then.

Ms Cowper takes this all in

Ms Cowper You say you've been using every way to cheat our system?
Eric Yes, I'll plead guilty and hopefully get a shorter sentence.
Ms Cowper Shorter sentence? I think prison would be a terrible waste of your talents, Mr Swan — you can start work for the Department on Monday.
Norman He can?
Eric I can?
Ms Cowper You're just the sort of man we've been looking for — Assistant Fraud Inspector.

Ms Cowper offers her hand and Eric shakes it

Norman (*to Eric*) You jammy basket!

Ms Cowper Yes, a Jammy Basket, that should go nicely with your heartless
    tart and Callus Wine. I'll see you at nine o'clock sharp.
Eric (*stunned and delighted*) Yes, of course, Ms Cowper. I'll be there.
Ms Cowper Good man.

*Ms Cowper squeezes Eric's "boobs" the same way he squeezed hers. Then
Norman's, then she gooses the two of them*

Eric   ⎫
                ⎬ (*together*) Whe-hey!
Norman   ⎭
Eric Fabulous, ay Norman? You get married on Saturday, I start work on
    Monday! What a weekend! (*He runs ahead of Ms Cowper to open the door
    for her*) After you, Ms Cowper.

*Eric opens the door, revealing Jenkins, frazzled and smouldering, his
clothes, face and hair blackened and his briefcase turned to charcoal,
smoke gently wafting off him*

The kitchen door opens with George and the washing machine. And — —

*Forbright and Sally enter through the front door with Dr Chapman on the
trolley*

The CURTAIN *falls*

FURNITURE AND PROPERTY LIST

Further dressing may be added at the director's discretion

ACT I

On stage: Working bay window. *On it:* curtains
Window-seat. *In it:* cricket bat, stump and other cricket equipment, foam mattress (optional)
Umbrella stand. *In it:* short umbrella, walking stick
Small cupboard. *In it:* large cardboard box. *In it:* long blonde wig, lady's corset, floral maternity dress, pair of blue stockings, large maternity bra
Sofa
Small table. *On it:* push-button phone
Chair
Paintings
Clock

Off stage: Mug of coffee (**Linda**)
Cordless phone (**Eric**)
Handbag. *In it:* door keys (**Linda**)
Woollen blanket (**Norman**)
Bottle of aspirin (**Norman**)
Clipboard (**Jenkins**)
Briefcase. *In it:* thin file of papers, thick folder with multi-coloured papers, reports and forms, pen (**Jenkins**)
Tray. *On it:* tea and Jaffa Cakes (**Eric**)
Cup of tea (**Jenkins**)
Plate. *On it:* Jaffa Cake (**Jenkins**)
Cardboard box (**George**)
Dining-room, kitchen, and bathroom keys (**Norman**)
Cup of tea (**Linda**)
Notebook and pen (**Dr Chapman**)
Bundle of clothes (**Norman**)

Personal: **Eric**: wedding ring
Eric: scrap of paper in pocket
George: wrist-watch
Norman: wrist-watch
Linda: wedding ring

ACT II

On stage: As in Act I

Off stage: Blanket (from Act I) **(Forbright)**
                 Large half-filled rubbish bag **(Norman)**
                 Sherry glass **(Jenkins)**
                 Table-cloths **(Sally)**
                 Sherry bottle **(Jenkins)**
                 Wooden mallet **(Jenkins)**
                 Foam **(Jenkins)**
                 Briefcase **(Ms Cowper)**
                 Trolley. *On it:* Stretcher with three straps **(Sally** and **Forbright)**
                 Long sheet **(Sally** and **Forbright)**
                 Tray. *On it:* Glasses of sherry **(Eric)**
                 Dummy stretcher (identical to original) **(Sally** and **Forbright)**
                 Decanter of brandy **(Brenda)**
                 Washing machine
                 Rubber plunger **(Jenkins)**
                 Foam-covered shirt

Personal: Engagement ring **(Brenda)**

LIGHTING PLOT

Property fittings required: nil
Interior. The same scene throughout

ACT I

To open: Full general lighting

ACT II

To open: Full general lighting

Cue 1	**Eric** opens his mouth to speak *The lights dim; flash of lightning*	(Page 91)
Cue 2	**Norman:** "... the same place twice!" *Flash of lightning*	(Page 92)

EFFECTS PLOT

At intermittent moments throughout the play, rain is visible both streaming down the window and falling outside the front door when it is opened

ACT I

To open:	Rain effect commences	
Cue 1	**Norman**: "Everybody does. I did." *Doorbell chimes*	(Page 6)
Cue 2	**Norman**: "I'll get it." *Doorbell chimes*	(Page 6)
Cue 3	**Norman**: "I beg your pardon?" *Phone rings*	(Page 30)
Cue 4	**Norman** locks the kitchen door *Phone rings*	(Page 31)
Cue 5	**Eric**: "Just keep her locked up." *Phone rings*	(Page 34)
Cue 6	**Eric** and **Jenkins** exit *Phone rings*	(Page 35)

ACT II

Cue 7	**Eric** backs out of the kitchen *Bubbles effect*	(Page 70)
Cue 8	**Eric**: "Uncle George?" *Doorbell rings*	(Page 75)
Cue 9	**Dr Chapman**: "Excuse me." *Doorbell rings*	(Page 75)
Cue 10	**Eric** throws the sherries *Crashing glass in dining-room*	(Page 81)